100 Days, 100 Letters

AMERICAN VALUES
RELIGIOUS VOICES

AMERICAN VALUES
RELIGIOUS VOICES
100 Days, 100 Letters

About the University of Cincinnati Press

The University of Cincinnati Press is committed to publishing rigorous, peer reviewed, leading scholarship accessibly to stimulate dialog and erase disciplinary boundaries between the academy, public intellectuals and lay practitioners. Building on the university's long-standing tradition of social responsibility, the press publishes books on topics which expose and resolve disparities at every level of society and have local, national and global impact.

University of Cincinnati Press, Cincinnati 45221
© 2019

ISBN 978-1-947602-40-3 (hardback)
ISBN 978-1-947602-41-0 (e-book, PDF)

Library of Congress Cataloging-in-Publication data

Weiss, Andrea L. and Lisa M. Weinberger, editors.
American values, religious voices : 100 days, 100 letters / edited by Andrea L. Weiss and Lisa M. Weinberger.
Cincinnati : University of Cincinnati Press, 2019. | Identifiers: LCCN 2018034409 (print) | LCCN 2018041311 (ebook) | ISBN 9781947602410 (Ebook, PDF) | ISBN 9781947602403 (hardback)
LCSH: United States—Religion—Miscellanea. | Values—United States—Miscellanea. | United States—Politics and government,—2017—Miscellanea. | Political culture—United States—History—21st century—Miscellanea. | Letters. | Public opinion—United States. | Trump, Donald, 1946–
LCC BL2525 (ebook) | LCC BL2525 .A547 2018 (print) | DDC 200.973—dc23
LC record available at https://lccn.loc.gov/2018034409

Designed and produced for UC Press by Masters Group Design • Philadelphia
Printed in the United States of America

First Printing

IN MEMORY

MAY 19, 1964–MAY 5, 2018

Rabbi Aaron D. Panken, PhD
President
Hebrew Union College–Jewish Institute of Religion

★ CONTENTS ★

American Values

8

LETTERS ON

EMPATHY

LETTERS 1, 13, 17, 36, 44, 52, 84, 92

12

LETTERS ON

EQUALITY

LETTERS 3, 12, 13, 17, 21, 25, 50, 74, 78, 85, 86, 100

11

LETTERS ON

DIVERSITY

LETTERS 2, 7, 29, 45, 62, 66, 71, 82, 83, 96, 100

22

LETTERS ON THE

VULNERABLE

LETTERS 1, 4, 6, 9, 16, 23, 24, 26, 30, 32, 40, 48, 51, 54, 56, 58, 75, 81, 82, 83, 93, 100

13

LETTERS ON

MERCY

LETTERS 1, 5, 33, 45, 47, 51, 54, 57, 63, 64, 87, 89, 92

24

LETTERS ON
FREEDOM

36

LETTERS ON
JUSTICE

12

LETTERS ON
PLURALISM

13

LETTERS ON
RESPONSIBILITY

17

LETTERS ON
PEACE

American Values

9

LETTERS ON THE

COMMON GOOD

LETTERS 2, 8, 11, 17, 18, 71, 91, 95, 100

15

LETTERS ON

HOSPITALITY

LETTERS 13, 16, 18, 31, 32, 35,
49, 51, 55, 58, 63, 64, 79, 82, 100

17

LETTERS ON

RESPECT

LETTERS 11, 24, 25, 28, 38, 45, 49, 50,
52, 53, 54, 62, 63, 73, 75, 77, 100

13

LETTERS ON

GENEROSITY

LETTERS 6, 16, 17, 27, 28, 33,
42, 69, 81, 84, 89, 91, 95

15

LETTERS ON

HUMILITY

LETTERS 1, 20, 21, 22, 40, 41, 42,
45, 52, 54, 69, 92, 95, 98, 100

RAISING 100 VOICES

By Andrea L. Weiss

On Thursday, November 10, 2016, two days after the election of Donald J. Trump, I walked into class at the Hebrew Union College–Jewish Institute of Religion (HUC-JIR) in New York City. Scheduled to teach about the biblical concept of "an eye for an eye," I quickly decided to scrap my lesson plan and instead share with my students the biblical texts I was thinking about on that day. I said to them: "We study Torah so that we can turn to our sacred texts at times like this, when we and those we serve need guidance, comfort, and support."

That class got me thinking about the role Bible scholars might be able to play at this moment in our nation's history, especially when many elected officials, like our vice president, publicly claim to bring a strong religious sensibility to their work. Throughout the tumultuous 2016 presidential campaign and in the wake of the election, I watched as many of the core values that had grounded and guided our country in the past were called into question or flagrantly disregarded: values like tolerance, inclusivity, and diversity, just to name a few.

An idea started to percolate: Could 100 scholars of sacred scripture be recruited to write letters articulating foundational American values rooted or reflected in our diverse religious traditions? What if they could send a letter a day to our president, vice president, and other leaders in Washington for the first 100 days of the new administration to remind them—and us—of who we are as a nation and how we should act moving forward?

At the time, I was eager to make progress on a book about metaphors for God in the Bible, and I possessed very few interfaith connections; so I had good reason to let this nascent idea go. Instead, I walked down the street and shared my scheme with my neighbor, Mark S. Smith, the Helena Professor of Old Testament Literature and Exegesis at Princeton Theological Seminary. When Mark, a mentor and distinguished Bible scholar, responded encouragingly and offered to help, I decided to explore the idea further.

A few days later, I had a chance to pitch my idea to HUC-JIR's president, Aaron D. Panken, who offered to fund the project. For Rabbi Panken, this project represented the type of "thought leadership" that was a pillar of his presidency. He encouraged his faculty to be engaged in key issues of our day and to bring our scholarship to bear on matters of concern in our contemporary world—just what the letter writing campaign aimed to accomplish.

The next week, while attending the Society of Biblical Literature and American Academy of Religion annual meetings in San Antonio, Texas, I shopped my idea around to as many scholars as possible. In a small notebook, I started collecting what would eventually become a list of 255 potential contributors.

At the same time, on November 16, 2016, I sent an email to my friend Lisa Weinberger, the creative director and founder of Masters Group Design in Philadelphia. Not quite realizing the scope of my request, I described my initial idea and asked: "Would you be willing to lend your design expertise?" Lisa responded right away: "I'm in."

Lisa and I met a few days after Thanksgiving with Elsie R. Stern, an old summer camp friend and vice president for academic affairs and associate professor of Bible at the Reconstructionist Rabbinical College. Sitting around Lisa's kitchen table, we came up with the campaign name:

AMERICAN VALUES RELIGIOUS VOICES
100 Days, 100 Letters

We then secured the domain name valuesandvoices.com. That gave us fifty-five days until the inauguration on January 20, 2017, to make this idea happen.

I quickly formed a multifaith advisory committee that included Deirdre Good (then theologian in residence at Trinity Church Wall Street), Herbert Marbury (associate professor of Bible and the ancient Near East at Vanderbilt University Divinity School), Hussein Rashid (founder of islamicate, L3C), Mark Smith, and Elsie Stern. The advisory committee finalized the contours of the project and sent out an initial round of nearly a hundred invitations. Over the course of the next month and a half—from early December until Day 1 of the campaign—we contacted 180 scholars until we finally secured our 100th letter writer.

Within days of our initial meeting, Lisa had created a visual identity. With the help of HUC-JIR rabbinic student interns Hilly Haber and Thalia Halpert Rodis, we established a social media presence on Twitter and Facebook, and later on Instagram. Lisa's creative team—Benjamin Brown, Vicki Gray-Wolfe, Matthew Muhlbaier, and Roni Lagin—joined the effort. They designed and built the website and, over time, created hundreds of visual assets to accompany the letters.

Early on, as the idea for this project took shape, I envisioned gathering photos of the 100 letter writers in a grid, as a way to celebrate the religious and racial diversity that has been a hallmark of our county. That image of 100 scholars is displayed on the homepage of the website (and on page 14), along with a statement that articulates the campaign's motivation:

Individually, it is hard to feel that one can have an impact on events unfolding around us. Collectively, we have the potential to speak truthfully and powerfully to those making critical decisions about our nation's future.

THE MECHANICS OF THE CAMPAIGN

Once the initial letters started to arrive in early January 2017, the editing phase began, and the first seven letters were selected for Week 1. Throughout the campaign, as I scheduled the letters a week at a time, I sought to offer a diverse selection of writers each week and also to respond in a timely manner to events as they transpired during the first few months of the Trump administration. Since the campaign began on a Friday—Inauguration Day on January 20, 2017—each Thursday on social media we posted a preview of the coming week's letter writers that listed each person's name, academic title, and institutional affiliation.

Day in and day out for fourteen weeks, at 5 a.m. eastern standard time, we electronically disseminated the day's letter in a variety of ways. With the help of MailChimp, we emailed the letters to our explicit audience: the president, vice president, members of the 115th Congress, and select members of the Trump administration. At the same time, the letter was uploaded to the website for our implicit audience: the more than two thousand subscribers who received an early morning email with a link to the letter, and the many others who learned about the letters through daily posts on our social media platforms (Facebook, Twitter, and Instagram). In addition, each day I mailed two printed and stamped letters, one addressed individually to the president and the other to the vice president.

Each week, we posted a schedule on social media with a preview of the upcoming letter writers.

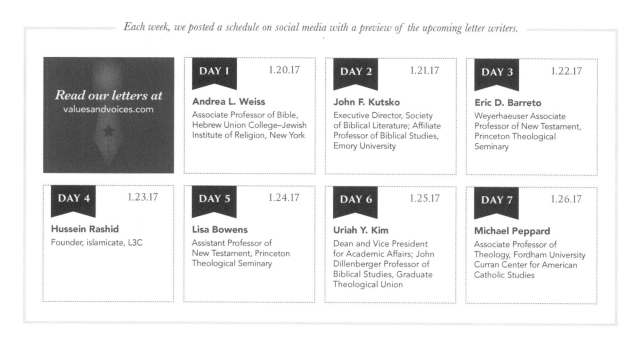

Read our letters at valuesandvoices.com

DAY 1   1.20.17
Andrea L. Weiss
Associate Professor of Bible, Hebrew Union College–Jewish Institute of Religion, New York

DAY 2   1.21.17
John F. Kutsko
Executive Director, Society of Biblical Literature; Affiliate Professor of Biblical Studies, Emory University

DAY 3   1.22.17
Eric D. Barreto
Weyerhaeuser Associate Professor of New Testament, Princeton Theological Seminary

DAY 4   1.23.17
Hussein Rashid
Founder, islamicate, L3C

DAY 5   1.24.17
Lisa Bowens
Assistant Professor of New Testament, Princeton Theological Seminary

DAY 6   1.25.17
Uriah Y. Kim
Dean and Vice President for Academic Affairs; John Dillenberger Professor of Biblical Studies, Graduate Theological Union

DAY 7   1.26.17
Michael Peppard
Associate Professor of Theology, Fordham University Curran Center for American Catholic Studies

THE LETTER WRITERS AND THEIR LETTERS

In the invitation sent to potential contributors, the advisory committee asked scholars from different faith communities the following questions: "What issues animate you at this particular moment in our nation's history? What passages from your religious tradition have you been thinking about in the wake of the election? How does your religious heritage speak to the matters that concern you most? What message—rooted in the texts you study and teach—would you most like to deliver to our national leaders and to a wider interfaith audience?"

We posed those questions to scholars of religion across the country, with the specification that all potential contributors possess a doctoral degree. In Letter 100, Elsie Stern captures the glorious diversity of the individuals who participated in the campaign: "We are men and women, from red states and blue states. We identify as African American, Asian, Latinx, Native American, and white. We are Buddhists, Christians of varied denominations, Hindus, Jews, Muslims, and Sikhs. Some of our families have been in this country since before it was 'America'; others are immigrants ourselves."

As contributors with varied religious backgrounds and diverse lived experiences responded in real time to the policies of the Trump administration and to President Trump, certain themes and religious texts gained prominence. Given the hostile attitude toward immigrants and refugees expressed on the campaign trail and reflected in early executive actions, it is no surprise that a sizable percentage of the letters contain scriptural teachings calling for the compassionate care of the vulnerable and a welcoming embrace of the stranger.

Given Trump's words and actions in the early days of his presidency, it is no surprise that nearly a quarter of the letters offer religious teachings on the topic of leadership. Given the focus of our nation's founding documents, it is no surprise that the word "justice" appears in almost one-third of the letters, often in conjunction with the word "liberty." Given the task of articulating a faith-based vision of American values, it is no surprise that many letter writers concentrated on subjects like love, equality, empathy, truth, and tolerance.

When we uploaded the letters onto the website, we tagged them by category in order to allow readers to search the letters by a theme.

THE AMERICAN DREAM		COMMON GOOD
TOLERANCE	COMPASSION	COMPROMISE
COURAGE	DEMOCRACY	DIGNITY	WISDOM
DIVERSITY	HOSPITALITY	PLURALISM
FREEDOM OF RELIGION		FREEDOM OF SPEECH
GENEROSITY	THE GOOD SAMARITAN	GRACE
GREATNESS	HAPPINESS	JUSTICE	HOPE
EMPATHY	HUMILITY	IMMIGRANTS	HONOR
KINDNESS	LEADERSHIP	RESPECT	LOVE
MERCY	NEIGHBORS	PEACE	EQUALITY
POWER	REFUGEES	LIBERTY	THE ENVIRONMENT
THE POOR	THE STRANGER	THE VULNERABLE
COMMUNITY	TRUTH	UNITY	DISSENT

Scholars drew upon a range of sources to address these topics. From the Hebrew Bible (or Old Testament), they most frequently cited the oft-repeated command to "not wrong or oppress the stranger" (Exodus 22:20 and elsewhere), as well as the charge to love both your neighbor and the stranger "as yourself" (Leviticus 19:18, 33–34). Numerous contributors quoted the creation story, with a particular focus on women and men being created in God's image (Genesis 1:26–27) and humans being appointed as caretakers of the earth (Genesis 1–2). Authors turning to the New Testament most often referred to Jesus' teaching about the treatment of "the least of these" in Matthew 25:31–46 and to lessons from the Sermon on the Mount (mainly from Matthew 5). Muslim contributors quoted a combined twenty passages from the Qur'an, with several references to 49:13: "We made you different nations and tribes that you may come to know one another." Hindu scholars cited several Sanskrit sources, including the Bhagavad Gita and Ramayana, while other authors discussed Buddhist teachings, a Sikh prayer, various rabbinic texts, and additional ancient writings. Contributors repeatedly mentioned concepts and phrases from the Declaration of Independence, the Great Seal of the United States, the Pledge of Allegiance, and the Statue of Liberty. In addition, they quoted a range of more contemporary figures, like Mahatma Gandhi, Irving Berlin, Martin Luther King Jr., Langston Hughes, Cesar Chavez, and Ronald Reagan. (See the indexes in the back of the book for a list of subjects and sources found in the letters.)

Like the topics covered and the sources utilized, the tone of the letters varies. Some letters offer advice or admonition, while others contain prayers or pleas. Some letters convey a sense of outrage or urgency, while others provide a modicum of optimism or a forceful reassurance of the enduing wisdom and moral vision preserved in our sacred texts. Many letters ask questions:

"What do we tell our daughters?"
Kimberly Russaw, Letter 12

"Will you be able to discern the wise and prescient voices among the cacophony of advice you receive?"
Corrine Carvalho, Letter 22

"Mr. President, what really is your vision for America?"
Mark S. Smith, Letter 28

"What can we do to create light together?"
Murali Balaji, Letter 36

"What would it mean…to call to mind our own experiences…and to empathize with a new generation of migrants and refugees?"
Judith Plaskow, Letter 44

"As elected officials in whom we have placed our trust, which path will you take to fulfill this higher calling?"
Tazim R. Kassam, Letter 91

...... ☆ ......

Reflecting on the multiple messages and moods exhibited in the 100 letters, Elsie Stern writes: "Yet, despite this diversity, our letters call attention to the same values: justice, compassion, protection of the vulnerable, hospitality, equal rights, and respect for all people, regardless of gender, race, religion, or status. Our writers have prayed that you will govern with wisdom and humility, putting the common good above individual concerns. In our diversity, we agree that these are the American values that must guide us as a nation."

.... ❝ ....

This project aims to contribute constructively to our national discourse, reaffirming who we are as Americans and modeling how we can learn from one another and work together for the common good.

....

WHAT THE CAMPAIGN ACCOMPLISHED

From the outset, the advisory committee explained to potential contributors what American Values, Religious Voices was attempting to accomplish: "This project aims to contribute constructively to our national discourse, reaffirming who we are as Americans and modeling how we can learn from one another and work together for the common good."

Feedback we received during the campaign proved that the letters achieved this goal. On Day 20, a follower wrote: "I am loving my daily inspirational letters from voices I am not accustomed to hearing." A few days later, a contributor relayed a conversation with a member of her church, a Manhattan Democrat who during the campaign had stopped speaking to his brother, a staunch Republican in Tulsa, Oklahoma. The

THESE LETTERS HAVE BEEN …
an anchor

THESE LETTERS HAVE BEEN …
a beacon of level-headedness and morality

THESE LETTERS HAVE BEEN …
a lifeline

THESE LETTERS HAVE BEEN …
an archive of compassion and democracy

THESE LETTERS HAVE BEEN …
a prayer

letters provided a means of reconciliation and, in his own words, "created dialogue and healing." Another reader described how the letters provided "living waters of sustenance and courage from deep ancient wells." Others characterized the campaign as an "archive of compassion and democracy" and "a beacon of level-headedness and morality."

These voices and many more testify to the impact the project had on a wide general audience. But did any of those directly addressed in the letters respond? Although we sent the president and vice president 100 printed and electronic letters, we received no response from the White House. Although we emailed 100 letters to the chiefs of staff and legislative directors serving 441 members of the House of Representatives and 100 members of the Senate (an initial list of 1,023 congressional staffers), we heard from only one individual.

On February 12, 2017, Katherine McGuire, chief of staff for Illinois Republican Congressman Randy Hultgren, sent an email challenging the concluding sentence of Letter 24 by Bryan Massingale. She expressed disappointment in the way the letter about our "house divided" ended by directly addressing the president and holding him responsible for healing the divisions in our nation. McGuire observed that "the conclusion seemed to press for continued divide" instead of "driving home that we—the nation's people—should do all we can to rise above our current selves and create again that important notion of 'together.'" In response, Massingale explained in an email that since the president "wields enormous symbolic power . . . the quality of the nation's public discourse will depend greatly on Mr. Trump's example and the kind of respect he grants to those who disagree with him."

More meaningful than the substance of this exchange is the mere fact of its existence, a point Massingale made when he wrote: "If only this kind of dialogue was the norm. We can only hope, pray, and continue to work toward that end." In a follow-up email, McGuire provided a welcome message of encouragement, especially in the early days of campaign: "Keep the letters coming. People are reading them. They help to make sense of the world we live in today and remind us of the world we all want to live in tomorrow."

HOW THIS BOOK WORKS

This book collects the 100 letters (some slightly edited for publication), arranged in ten sections. Each section begins with a listing of the authors who appear in the letters that follow.

☆ *Read the letters sequentially,* as they appeared when the campaign took place from January 20 to April 29, 2017.

☆ *Explore the letters by topic or by author* using the list of authors in the table of contents, the American values highlighted on pages 8–11, or the indexes beginning on pg. 162. This will allow you to put the letters and the letter writers in conversation with one another, connecting diverse faith traditions and sacred texts, comparing what different religions have to say about issues that matter, creating dialogues that bring people together around core American and religious values.

More than merely words on paper, these 100 letters can enlighten and inspire us, reaffirming who we are as a nation and guiding how we should act as individuals, one among many.

THE VALUE OF DESIGN

By Lisa M. Weinberger

After the divisive and vitriolic presidential campaign of 2016, I felt hopeless. I craved a dialogue centered on what I value as an American: tolerance, respect, empathy, and hope. Unfortunately, the only exchanges I encountered were the hostile posts and tweets that flooded my social media feeds for months. There was no real dialogue, just screaming. Everyone was so firmly anchored on one side or the other that any effort to bring America's diversity together—to highlight what makes us truly great—seemed improbable.

It was not until my friend Andrea Weiss proposed the idea of creating a nonpartisan unity campaign that I saw any hope for an exchange that could be healthy and maybe even healing. I needed it. We *all* needed it.

Andrea's idea was to gather together 100 voices representing people of not just different religions, but of different races, genders, ages, political affiliations, sexual orientations, and geography. This seemed promising. All scholars of religion, the letter writers would use their unique perspectives to facilitate a meaningful conversation about what unites us as Americans.

When Andrea told me she needed help, I offered my services without hesitation. I believed that at such a vexing time in our nation's history, amplifying the voices of a collection of multifaith scholars could be a small step toward healing a divided nation. I wanted to be a part of that.

BRANDING THE CAMPAIGN

As a graphic designer, I craft visual identities for organizations that struggle to get noticed. I rely on design to create a platform to enhance their visibility and help others see them with clarity. The American Values, Religious Voices campaign was no different. It needed a platform—a visual expression—to symbolize its purpose. The goal was to generate engagement. The letters by themselves might not have been enough to attract attention to a dialogue that, to my knowledge, was unlike any previously presented to the public. My job was to create the visual arena in which this conversation could take place.

Campaign color palette, primary typeface, and graphics

TRAJAN PRO

We had less than two months before the first letter was scheduled to arrive in Washington. I moved swiftly to establish the visuals. I quickly landed on a familiar American color palette and then created the official symbol of the effort. It was a bookmark icon meant to reference the religious texts that inspired the letters. In the middle of the bookmark, the full campaign name was presented with a nod to what would later become the shorthand social media handle (@ValuesAndVoices) and hashtag (#valuesandvoices). The graphic would be emblazoned on the campaign website, social media profiles, electronic communication, and even buttons and coffee mugs.

In short order, the identity was threaded through all the communication vehicles, creating a unified campaign brand. I developed a set of social media assets to help count down the campaign launch, and my work was done—or so I thought.

Letter 1 was released, kicking off the need for our rapid-fire visual response to an evolving campaign, something for which we could never have planned. The design component took on a life of its own for 100 straight days. Luckily, I am surrounded by a creative team of designers at Masters Group Design who were willing to lend their talents to the growing opportunities for campaign exposure.

BUILDING AWARENESS

The day-to-day strategy to build awareness involved promoting each author and drawing attention to the key message in each letter. We did this in a variety of ways, including developing daily images featuring a brief quote from that day's letter. We tweeted and posted these inspiring takeaways on Facebook and Instagram. These powerful insights

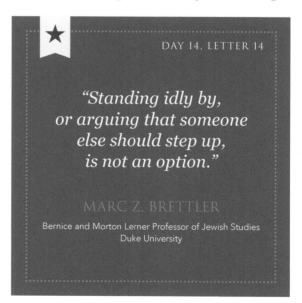

DAY 14, LETTER 14

"Standing idly by, or arguing that someone else should step up, is not an option."

MARC Z. BRETTLER

Bernice and Morton Lerner Professor of Jewish Studies
Duke University

also provided a preview of the letters, encouraging followers to see the full text on our site. Our Instagram

►■ @VALUESANDVOICES ■◄

features all 100 quotes and frames the campaign like a visual diary.

We designed weekly schedules to showcase the seven authors whose letters were coming up (page 15). We posted them on social media to build anticipation and allow the authors and their networks time to get the word out. Shares and retweets confirmed that news about the letters was spreading.

GRAPHICS THAT SPEAK

As soon as the website went live, we immediately began receiving feedback. For example, on Day 3 a United Methodist Sunday school teacher wrote to tell us how she planned to use the letters with her students. This email and a mounting collection of comments from across the country added a new dimension to the campaign. We had not expected this. People were actively participating in the dialogue and connecting to the values and voices we were magnifying. Those responses needed to be shared as an integral part of the campaign's narrative. Our solution was to create graphic images for many of the comments and highlight them on social media. Some designs showcased words of gratitude, while others testified to the personal impact the campaign was having on readers. (See Lia Howard's essay on page 146 for more about this feedback.)

We also developed graphics to mark holidays such as Valentine's Day, Presidents' Day, International Women's Day, and Passover (pages 49, 61, 109, and 121).

AT A TIME WHEN POLITICAL (AND THEOLOGICAL) DISCOURSE TENDS TO BE UNTHOUGHTFUL, UNPRODUCTIVE, AND UNCHARITABLE, THIS PROJECT STRIKES THE RIGHT TONE.

It truly is a gift.

They were used in social media posts that linked the holidays to the letters. The graphic images, in essence, became a form of advertising that created continuous access to the collection long after the letters were first posted.

Once the letters started appearing on the website, I transitioned from being not only a part of the team but also an audience member. Like thousands of other subscribers, I woke up every morning to the newest letter in my inbox. I found myself completely engaged: reading, learning, questioning, and feeling myself moved by the richness of perspectives. Then one morning I read Kimberly Russaw's urgent message in Letter 12 (page 40). The letter ends with a charge to our elected officials to "lead, craft policy, and legislate" in a way that would "affirm for all our daughters the core biblical principle that they are 'awesomely and wonderfully made' (Psalm 139:14)." This message really resonated with me. As a vision of an "awesome girl" started to take shape in my mind, I talked to my design partners about my plan to illustrate the letter's message (page 37). They were eager to follow suit. What resulted was a series of illustrations, each responding visually to parts of the letters that moved us as designers and campaign followers.

My team generated over 180 graphic images during the three-month campaign. We used them to invite new audiences in and encourage people to join the conversation about our shared values. Long after the 100th day, the graphics became a tool the campaign could use to continue calling attention to the letters on social media and to show how they connected to the latest news. For example, on September 6, 2017, when the end of DACA (the Deferred Action for Childhood Arrivals program) seemed imminent, we posted Benjamin Brown's illustration "America's Open Door" (page 121) on Facebook. We cited quotes from seven letters that highlighted religious teachings with a message about treating the vulnerable with compassion. On June 20, 2018, as news spread about the separation of children from their parents at the border, we posted Vicki Gray-Wolfe's illustration "Refugee Boy" (page 97). The image had been inspired more than a year earlier by Ellen Armour's Letter 9 (page 35), in which she writes: "No one is more vulnerable than refugees, those who are forced to give up all that they have and all they know in order to travel—often long distances and at great danger—in search of safety." The current situation made this illustration even more poignant and heart-wrenching. The tweet reminded our followers that "our different religious traditions demand that we care for all people created in God's image—especially the 'least of these' (Matthew 25:40)—and 'be good to . . . the orphans and the needy' (Qur'an 4:36)."

ASSESSING THE CAMPAIGN'S IMPACT

It has been over a year since our patriotic package of letters was delivered to more than five hundred leaders in Washington and presented on our website. Unfortunately, there is no way to quantify how many people read the letters or otherwise encountered our authors' words. We had tangible evidence that during the 100 days, over two thousand people subscribed to the letters online; and, by the end of that time, we had received over fifty thousand visits to the website. The largest segment of our readership came from the United States, but individuals from Canada, the United Kingdom, Israel, India, Australia, Germany, and Kenya also visited the website. This campaign about American values had traveled from coast to coast and well beyond our borders.

From my perspective, this project was never about reaching a magic number of readers. It was about facilitating a civil dialogue about core American values at a turbulent moment. And it was about an unlikely partnership between a biblical scholar and a graphic designer that formed because the times demanded it. This collaboration resulted in a collection of 100 letters that, as one reader described them, stand as "positive reminders of who we are and encouragement to live boldly rather than out of fear." The most meaningful summary of the contribution of our collective words and graphics came from another follower who wrote:

"Let no one say there was silence."

**T**HESE LETTERS ARE NOT ONLY INSPIRATIONAL, THEY ARE A HISTORICAL RECORD OF OUR TIME.

American Values, Religious Voices reader Rabbi Amy R. Perlin

The Letters

RELIGIOUS VOICES: DAY 1–10

LETTER 1 | JANUARY 20, 2017

Andrea L. Weiss

Jack, Joseph and Morton Mandel
Provost & Associate Professor of Bible,
Hebrew Union College–Jewish Institute
of Religion

LETTER 2 | JANUARY 21, 2017

John F. Kutsko

Executive Director, Society of Biblical
Literature & Affiliate Professor of Biblical
Studies, Emory University

LETTER 3 | JANUARY 22, 2017

Eric D. Barreto

Weyerhaeuser Associate Professor of
New Testament, Princeton Theological
Seminary

LETTER 4 | JANUARY 23, 2017

Hussein Rashid

Independent Scholar & Founder,
islamicate, L3C

LETTER 5 | JANUARY 24, 2017

Lisa Bowens

Assistant Professor of New Testament,
Princeton Theological Seminary

LETTER 6 | JANUARY 25, 2017

Uriah Y. Kim

Dean and Vice President for Academic
Affairs & John Dillenberger Professor of
Biblical Studies, Graduate Theological
Union

LETTER 7 | JANUARY 26, 2017

Michael Peppard

Associate Professor of Theology, Curran
Center for American Catholic Studies,
Fordham University

LETTER 8 | JANUARY 27, 2017

Jean-Pierre Ruiz

Associate Professor of Theology and
Religious Studies, St. John's University

LETTER 9 | JANUARY 28, 2017

Ellen T. Armour

E. Rhodes and Leona B. Carpenter
Associate Professor of Theology,
Vanderbilt University Divinity School

LETTER 10 | JANUARY 29, 2017

Bill J. Leonard

James and Marilyn Dunn Professor of
Baptist Studies & Professor of Church
History, Wake Forest University

Dear President Trump, Vice President Pence, Members of the Trump Administration and the 115th Congress,

At this time of transition in our nation's history, the words of the Bible call to us with clarity and urgency, reminding us of the core values that have formed the foundation of American society in the past and should guide us now as we begin a new administration.

In the book *Reading the Bible with the Founding Fathers*, Daniel L. Dreisbach documents the Bible's profound influence on American politics and culture in the eighteenth and early nineteenth centuries. Records show that figures like George Washington, Thomas Paine, and John Adams invoked the words of the prophet Micah: "God has told you . . . what is good, and what God requires of you: only to do justice, and to love mercy, and to walk humbly with your God" (Micah 6:8). Explaining the popularity of this frequently quoted verse, Dreisbach writes: "A commonplace belief among the founding generation was that both individual and collective righteousness were prerequisites for divine favor and vital to the success of the American political experiment." They believed that "a self-governing people must have an internal moral compass that would encourage individual citizens and the broader society to behave in a controlled, disciplined manner."

The message of Micah 6:8 echoes throughout the Hebrew Bible, teaching us what it means "to do justice and to love mercy." The book of Exodus commands: "You shall not wrong or oppress a stranger, for you were strangers in the land of Egypt. You shall not mistreat any widow or orphan" (Exodus 22:20–21). Again and again, the Bible insists that we safeguard the most vulnerable individuals in our midst and treat them with dignity and empathy. The prophets voice this expectation loud and clear, as when Isaiah instructs: "Cease to do evil; learn to do good. Devote yourself to justice. Aid the wronged. Uphold the rights of the orphan. Defend the cause of the widow" (Isaiah 1:16–17).

> *. . . these ancient biblical teachings about justice and mercy should dictate how we act and determine the policies we enact.*

Still today, in the early twenty-first century, these ancient biblical teachings about justice and mercy should dictate how we act and determine the policies we enact. Together, let us work to preserve and make manifest the values upon which our democracy was founded.

Dear President Trump, Vice President Pence, Members of the Trump Administration and the 115th Congress,

The country was knit together like a quilt by compromise. It was the defining quality of those who composed America's sacred contract, the Constitution of the United States of America. Compromise is a powerful word—a mark of wisdom, not weakness.

The main ingredient in America's melting pot is pluralism, and this is possible only through compromise. How else can we find common ground and common good in a country as diverse as the United States? Compromise is the art of great and lasting deals in business, politics, communities, and religion.

The Bible teaches us the virtue of compromise; and that is meaningful in a country with deep beliefs in sacred texts. For example, the first five books of the Old Testament were composed by a community not unlike our own, one facing great challenges and differences. In response, at least four religious parties—twice as many as our two-party system—banded together and wove their stories to form one inspiring narrative. Instead of seeking to beat each other, or to ban the other, they joined to form a more perfect union.

> *Compromise is a powerful word—a mark of wisdom, not weakness.*

There is no single Bible. As complex as the country is, as diverse its citizens, so, too, is the Bible. Jews, Orthodox Christians, Catholics, and Protestants each have different Bibles with different books. And these unique collections include books with very different points of view. The Bible, like democracy, cultivates competing ideas. The Bible teaches that alternative viewpoints coexist in healthy communities. The diversity in each tradition's Bible models the principle that the whole is greater than the sum of its parts. Our country's motto is *e pluribus unum*, "out of many, one."

I encourage you to value diversity, to draw from the deep gene pool of America that fuels creativity and imagination, to promote pluralism, to encourage debate, and to lead with the strength of compromise.

Dear President Trump, Vice President Pence, Members of the Trump Administration and the 115th Congress,

At their best, our religious traditions can point us to wisdom in moments of great uncertainty, comfort in times of grief, inspiration to act and speak when we would wish to hide in fear.

> *At their best, our religious traditions can point us to wisdom in moments of great uncertainty, comfort in times of grief, inspiration to act and speak when we would wish to hide in fear.*

At its best, this country has stood for revolutionary ideals:
• The freedom to speak, protest, and worship;
• The transformative belief that all of God's children are created equal;
• The hope that, as Dr. King showed us, "the arc of the moral universe is long, but it bends toward justice."

It is in this spirit of belief and hope that I write.

At our best, Americans have been salt and light in the world. But, Mr. President, we know that we are not always at our best. Our collective histories are full of grave errors alongside shining examples of good news and grace. We fail. We fall short of our ideals. We harm others. We mistake prosperity for progress. We tend to misname privilege and call it a blessing. That is, we all are liable to sin, and our sinfulness is never just personal. Our sins reverberate in our neighborhoods, our nation, our world.

But Jesus and his church have taught me this good news: the reconciliation and repair of relationships we have broken do not rest merely on our good intentions or even our hard work. Instead, it is God's grace that transforms the world. That grace infuses our frail efforts toward justice with the power of new, abundant life. Such transformations have happened before in this country: in the movements for women's suffrage, for the undoing of Jim Crow, for marriage equality.

And so, I would exhort you to lean on that good news, not as a way to "let go and let God," but as a deep wisdom we all must learn anew every day. Rest on the gift of God's grace and the courage of prophets and protesters to inspire policymaking that will make a real difference. Let that good news inspire your words, your actions, even your tweets, to reflect what has been best about our country.

Dear President Trump, Vice President Pence, Members of the Trump Administration and the 115th Congress,

Muslims have been part of this country since its founding. Since nearly a third of all slaves were Muslim, this country literally was built on the backs of Muslims. We have remained important contributors to American history, serving to defend our nation and contributing culturally to what it means to be American. Thomas Jefferson's copy of the Qur'an sits in the Library of Congress as a testament to how important Muslim thought was to the founding of this country.

> *Thomas Jefferson's copy of the Qur'an sits in the Library of Congress as a testament to how important Muslim thought was to the founding of this country.*

The Qur'an argues forcefully for religious freedom (2:256) and encourages people of different faiths to compete with each other in doing good in the world (2:148). The Qur'an also speaks lovingly of Christ's message (chapter 19); and it repeatedly reminds us that we have obligations to take care of the most vulnerable in our society: to "give away some of [our] wealth, however much [we] cherish it . . . to orphans, the needy, travelers and beggars" (2:177).

Imam Ali, the successor to the Prophet Muhammad's authority over the community, writes a letter to Malik al-Ashtar, the man he appointed as the governor of Egypt (c. 658). This letter is a manifestation of ethical and just leadership, which explains why, 1,400 years later, United Nations Secretary-General Kofi Annan referenced it in connection to the Universal Declaration of Human Rights.

Imam Ali's letter offers several important lessons for any leader seeking to unite people working for a greater good. Some of the points that may be of greatest importance to you are: All people are of one creation; differences are divinely ordained, so they should not be punished. Forgive, because God is forgiving. Do not act rashly, and always seek multiple courses of action. Focus on justice. Remember the common people over the elites, because they are the ones who are the base of any society. Appoint to the head of your army someone who is slow to anger, quick to forgive, and avoids violence as a solution. Pay attention to those who have no access to you. Always set time aside to think, reflect, and remember God.

The president of the United States of America is responsible for all Americans, with liberty and justice for all.

DAY 5, LETTER 5

Lisa Bowens

Dear President Trump, Vice President Pence, Members of the Trump Administration and the 115th Congress,

This monumental moment of change in this country's history necessitates reflection upon scripture in light of our nation's past, present, and future. At the heart of Christian faith is the belief that the Messiah has come, and that we are called to bear witness to Jesus' birth, death, and resurrection in the midst of a suffering world. How do we do this?

In Luke's Gospel, Jesus announces the two greatest commandments: Love God with all your heart, soul, strength, and mind; and love your neighbor as yourself (Luke 10:25–37). By juxtaposing these two commandments, Jesus insists that loving God is inextricably linked to loving your neighbor. We display love for God by the treatment of our neighbors, and we can love our neighbors because of our love for God.

After speaking these words Jesus is asked, "Who is my neighbor?" He responds by telling the story of the good Samaritan who assists the victim of a violent crime. Through this parable, Luke teaches that a neighbor can be someone from a different ethnic group or someone with different beliefs, even someone considered an "outsider." Christians bear witness to Christ's advent by treating others—particularly the "other"—with love, compassion, and mercy. Religious texts from other faith traditions espouse similar principles.

> *. . . loving God is inextricably linked to loving your neighbor.*

In our nation's history, America has often ignored Scripture's voice, as evidenced in the treatment of Native Americans and the enslavement of African Americans. At such junctures, our leaders divided these two commandments, professing to love God but rejecting the call to love one's neighbor. Yet we also have witnessed moments of divine grace–filled interruptions, when love of both God and neighbor prevailed, such as in the abolitionist and civil rights movements.

If this nation is a Christian nation, as many claim it to be, then we stand once again at the precipice of decision. Will we divorce love of God from love of neighbor, or will we embody both of these commandments in our laws, actions, behavior, and words? The Christ event, the Messiah's presence, beckons us to do the latter.

Dear President Trump, Vice President Pence, Members of the Trump Administration and the 115th Congress,

Like millions of immigrants who preceded her, my mother believed that giving up her life in her native country would bring incomparable opportunities to her children in America. She came to the United States in the early 1970s and to this day has not once visited her homeland. I am a son of this woman who believed in the American Dream.

> *. . . America is great not only because of its power, but more so because of its generosity and compassion.*

Like my mother, I also believed in the American Dream; but I had my doubts as to whether I would ever be accepted and perceived as an American rather than as a perpetual stranger. It was during such a time of doubt in my youth when President Ronald Reagan shared a letter he received before he left office: "You can go to live in France, but you cannot become a Frenchman. You can go to live in Germany or Turkey or Japan, but you cannot become a German, a Turk, or a Japanese. But anyone, from any corner of the Earth, can come to live in America and become an American." You can imagine how relieved and happy I was to know that the president of the United States agreed with the idea that the United States is where foreigners not only can be welcomed but also can become Americans.

In my humble opinion, as someone who follows the teachings of Jesus Christ, America is great not only because of its power, but more so because of its generosity and compassion. Jesus taught that, in the end, nations and peoples will be judged not by what we say or believe, but by what we do for the most vulnerable in the world: the hungry, the stranger, the sick, the imprisoned (Matthew 25:31–46). In fact, Jesus says that when we do not welcome strangers and do not help the least among our communities, we are actually rejecting Jesus.

Millions have benefited from America's greatness in the past. I pray that as the president of the United States, you will continue to leave America's door open and care for all those already living in the United States.

Dear President Trump, Vice President Pence, Members of the Trump Administration and the 115th Congress,

The first time I saw a census form was as a young man doing genealogical research about my ancestors who fled Ireland during the Great Famine. At the Family History Library in Salt Lake City, when a volunteer showed me an early census from rural Illinois, I discovered what I needed to piece together my family tree. But I was surprised by something else about the census form. *Why did it not record my ancestors' religion?*

The librarian graciously explained why: In the United States, the government does not keep a record of the religious affiliations of private individuals. "It's a principle of religious freedom," she said, "and the potential for abuse of such records is too dangerous."

> *The story of America's religious diversity should always be written in our history books, but not in a census or registry.*

That Mormon librarian was right—and she would know. Her people were chased violently across the country, from New York to Ohio, Missouri, Illinois, and ultimately Utah. Mormons thus champion religious liberty as the core American value. So should we all.

My own religion, Roman Catholicism, does not have an unblemished history on this matter. But it is currently in full-throated support of religious liberty—and better late than never. We Catholics view religious liberty as a bipartisan issue. Like Mormons, Catholics remember well when we were outsiders in America. Hence we take to heart the scriptural teaching: "You shall not mistreat or oppress a stranger, for you once were strangers" (Exodus 22:21).

Today, it is often Muslims who are marginalized in America, even though there need be no conflict between being Muslim and being American. In fact, there were about as many Muslims already on our shores at the founding of our country as there were Catholics. Yet those early American Muslims, brought here first as slaves, do not often appear in our history books.

The story of America's religious diversity should always be written in our history books, but not in a census or registry. An individual's religion is not the government's business.

Mr. President, religious liberty demands that our government never register our fellow citizens by religion, nor allow surveillance on the basis of religious affiliation. To do either of these would be profoundly un-American, violating our sacred founding freedoms of religion and assembly.

Dear President Trump, Vice President Pence, Members of the Trump Administration and the 115th Congress,

Because I am a professor of biblical studies interested in the pervasive influence of the Bible on people's minds and hearts, I read the sermon delivered by Rev. Robert Jeffress on Inauguration Day with great interest, especially because he made reference to the book of Nehemiah.

As a young man, I was part of a group of religious leaders and grassroots organizers who took our inspiration from the pages of Nehemiah. In the New York neighborhoods of Brownsville and East New York, Nehemiah's ancient words rang true: "You see the trouble we are in, how Jerusalem lies in ruins with its gates burned. Come, let us rebuild the wall of Jerusalem, so that we may no longer suffer disgrace" (Nehemiah 2:17). To this, the people of Jerusalem responded, "Let us start building!" Then "they committed themselves to the common good" (Nehemiah 2:18) and together rebuilt their ruined city. Centuries later, the people of the interfaith community organization East Brooklyn Congregations likewise joined together to build affordable housing, an effort christened the Nehemiah Plan.

> *Together, then, let us start building—not walls but bridges, roads, and communities.*

Citing Nehemiah, Pastor Jeffress suggested that God smiles on you, Mr. President, and on the building of walls. Yes, God smiles on all of God's children, both the meek and the mighty. Yes, God calls on all of us to work together in building for the sake of the common good. Yet, as Pope Francis insists: "A person who thinks only about building walls, wherever they may be, and not building bridges, is not Christian."

President Reagan was the last U.S. president to speak forcefully about walls. Standing before the Brandenburg Gate during a 1987 visit to then-divided Berlin, he declared to Mikhail Gorbachev, leader of the Soviet Union: "We welcome change and openness; for we believe that freedom and security go together, that the advance of human liberty can only strengthen the cause of world peace . . . Mr. Gorbachev, open this gate. Mr. Gorbachev, tear down this wall!"

There is much to be done in our time, the sort of hard work on which God smiles because it is done for the sake of the dignity and the well-being of all God's creatures. Together, then, let us start building—not walls but bridges, roads, and communities.

Dear President Trump, Vice President Pence, Members of the Trump Administration and the 115th Congress,

Among the serious challenges confronting us today is a growing global refugee crisis. Fear of terrorism makes some wary of welcoming refugees into the United States. As a Christian theologian, I ask: What would Jesus do?

The answer, I believe, is clear from the Gospel accounts of who Jesus was, what he said, and what he did. Matthew tells us Jesus was born a refugee. His parents fled their hometown to protect him from a cruel king who sought his death (Matthew 2:13–15). Like Moses, another biblical refugee whose own birth narrative finds echoes here, Jesus became a respected religious leader, an itinerant teacher who preached and practiced care for the most vulnerable. Jesus blessed those who extended themselves and treated others with compassion: "I was hungry and you gave me something to eat, I was thirsty and you gave me something to drink, I was a stranger and you welcomed me" (Matthew 25:35).

May we . . . commit ourselves to greeting refugees with love and faith, rather than rejecting them with hate and fear.

Though other issues divide us, Jesus' example compels Christians of all stripes to join people of other faiths and become deeply involved in refugee resettlement programs across our country, including in my hometown of Nashville. Many in our area eagerly await the premiere of *All Saints*, a movie based on the true story of All Saints' Episcopal Church in nearby Smyrna, Tennessee. This small, dying congregation took the risk of welcoming in a group of refugees from Myanmar (Burma)—a decision that not only saved the refugees, but ended up saving the church.

No one is more vulnerable than refugees, those who are forced to give up all that they have and all they know in order to travel—often long distances and at great danger—in search of safety. May we—our elected officials and our fellow citizens alike—follow All Saints' example and commit ourselves to greeting refugees with love and faith, rather than rejecting them with hate and fear.

Dear President Trump, Vice President Pence, Members of the Trump Administration and the 115th Congress,

The Baptist tradition that I claim and that claims me began in religious dissent. Thomas Helwys, Baptist founder, resisted all attempts by government or state-privileged religions to coerce individual faith. In *A Short Declaration of the Mystery of Iniquity* (1612), he advised King James I that governments should permit all persons to "choose their religion themselves, seeing they only must stand themselves before the judgment seat of God . . . when it shall be no excuse for them to say, 'We were commanded or compelled to be of this religion by the king.' "

In 1636, when the Puritan religious establishment exiled Roger Williams, America's quintessential dissenter, into the "howling wilderness" of New England, he purchased land from the Narragansets and founded Providence (Rhode Island), the first colony to offer liberty to persons of differing religions or no religion at all. Williams called it "a shelter for persons distressed of conscience" and communicated his "purchase to loving friends . . . who desired to take shelter here with me."

> **Dissent remains perilous.**

Good citizenship, Williams insisted, was not limited to Christians, but "Jews, Turks [Muslims], or anti-Christians" could "be peaceable and quiet subjects, loving and helpful neighbours." Williams' legacy continued with eighteenth-century Virginia Baptist John Leland, who asserted that "Bible Christians and Deists" alike were free to resist "self-named Christians," those who tyrannized "the consciences of others, under the specious garb of religion and good order."

Across American history, such religious pluralism is often granted grudgingly, whether exiling Baptists, hanging Quakers, shooting Catholics and Mormons, jailing Jehovah's Witnesses, or burning churches, mosques, and synagogues along the way. Dissent remains perilous.

I hope that, under your leadership, the U.S. continues to endure as "a shelter for persons distressed of conscience." Those who prefer otherwise can blame the early Baptists.

Letter 12 moved Lisa Weinberger to create this "Awesome Girl" illustration.
Kimberly Russaw urges our leaders to make sure that "the way you lead, craft policy,
and legislate should affirm for all our daughters the core biblical principle that
they are 'awesomely and wonderfully made' (Psalm 139:14)."

RELIGIOUS VOICES: DAY 11–20

LETTER 11 | JANUARY 30, 2017

Eboo Patel
Founder and President, Interfaith
Youth Core

LETTER 12 | JANUARY 31, 2017

Kimberly D. Russaw
Assistant Professor of Hebrew Bible,
Christian Theological Seminary

LETTER 13 | FEBRUARY 1, 2017

Aristotle Papanikolaou
Professor of Theology & Archbishop
Demetrios Chair in Orthodox Theology
and Culture, Fordham University

LETTER 14 | FEBRUARY 2, 2017

Marc Z. Brettler
Bernice and Morton Lerner Professor
of Jewish Studies, Duke University

LETTER 15 | FEBRUARY 3, 2017

M. Craig Barnes
President & Professor of Pastoral Ministry,
Princeton Theological Seminary

LETTER 16 | FEBRUARY 4, 2017

Karina Martin Hogan
Associate Professor of Theology,
Fordham University

LETTER 17 | FEBRUARY 5, 2017

Anantanand Rambachan
Professor of Religion, Philosophy, and
Asian Studies, Saint Olaf College

LETTER 18 | FEBRUARY 6, 2017

Emilie M. Townes
Dean & E. Rhodes and Leona B.
Carpenter Professor of Womanist Ethics
and Society, Vanderbilt University
Divinity School

LETTER 19 | FEBRUARY 7, 2017

Carmen Nanko-Fernández
Professor of Hispanic Theology and
Ministry & Director of Hispanic
Theology and Ministry Program,
Catholic Theological Union

LETTER 20 | FEBRUARY 8, 2017

Shalom E. Holtz
Associate Professor of Bible,
Yeshiva University

Dear President Trump, Vice President Pence, Members of the Trump Administration and the 115th Congress,

I write as a proud American Muslim of Indian descent.

I believe every inch of America is sacred, from sea to shining sea. I believe we make it holy by whom we welcome and how we relate to each other. Call it my Muslim eyes on the American project: "We made you different nations and tribes that you may come to know one another," says the Qur'an (49:13). There is no better place on earth than America to enact that vision, a vision that is part of the very definition of our nation. Martin Luther King Jr. described the American dream this way, as "the dream of men of all races, creeds, national backgrounds, living together as brothers."

> "
> *Pluralism is not a birthright in America; it is a responsibility.*

I call this the dream of pluralism: the hope that people of various identities will be respected, that positive relationships between them will be nurtured, and that they will be inspired to work together to strengthen the common good. This dream recognizes that people will disagree. When this happens, we must treat each other as friends, not enemies, as the Qur'an teaches: "Argue with them in ways that are best and most gracious" (16:125).

This is the dream of democracy, a dream that must be encouraged by our laws and policies in order for it to manifest fully in our civic and cultural life. As Walt Whitman sang: "I say democracy is only of use there that it may pass on and come to its flower and fruit in manners, in the highest forms of interaction between men, and their beliefs—in religion, literature, colleges, and schools" (*Democratic Vistas*).

Pluralism is not a birthright in America; it is a responsibility. Pluralism does not fall from the sky or rise from the ground. People have fought for pluralism. People have kept the promise. People have worked hard to fulfill the dream. America is exceptional not because there is magic in our air, but because there is fierce determination in our citizens.

Every generation has to keep the American promise. Will you?

Dear President Trump, Vice President Pence, Members of the Trump Administration and the 115th Congress,

As we watch America erupt in the dawn of a Trump presidency, many people feel extremely vulnerable and are acting and reacting from positions of fear. I wince at the video of middle schoolers chanting, "Build a wall," while their peers cry and an adult stands helpless in the middle of the room. My back gets tight when I read the Facebook post of an African American mother whose son asked her if there would be slavery again with Trump as president. Amidst all of this, I have one question: What do we tell our daughters?

As a country, we elected a candidate whose campaign was fueled with misogyny, xenophobia, and physical aggression. We were bombarded with audio of a man boasting about grabbing women by their genitalia and reports of demeaning and hurtful comments said to and about women over the years. How can we align this historical reality with the biblical principle that "God created the human in God's image . . . male and female God created them" (Genesis 1:27)? How can we reconcile what we have seen and heard with the foundational scriptural idea that all of God's creations—women and men—are "very good" (Genesis 1:31)? Again, what do we tell our daughters?

> **What do we tell our daughters?**

In your position as president of the United States, I urge you to consider how your actions impact the lives of the young girls created *imago dei*, in God's image. We need you—through your words and actions—to tell our daughters that despite how they may feel and what they may experience, they are safe. Please square up your adult shoulders and tell our girls that no harm will come to them simply because of who and what they are. I urge you to work like our very lives depend on it (because they do!) in order to prevent policies and practices from being put in place that will chip away at the humanity and well-being of our daughters. Instead, the way you lead, craft policy, and legislate should affirm for all our daughters the core biblical principle that they are "awesomely and wonderfully made" (Psalm 139:14).

Dear President Trump, Vice President Pence, Members of the Trump Administration and the 115th Congress,

One of the foundational teachings of the Orthodox Christian Church is that all humans are made in the image and likeness of God (Genesis 1:26–27). Such a teaching resonates with foundational principles of the United States of America: that all humans are endowed by their Creator with inalienable rights and dignity.

> *Rather than a politics of divisiveness, please consider moving our country toward a politics of empathy . . .*

After one of the most divisive elections in U.S. history, I appeal to you to assure the American people that your presidency will continue to move our country forward toward the realization of our core principles: that all human beings must be affirmed as unique and irreplaceable. I ask that you use the power of the presidency to honor and value all Americans, over half of whom are women. I urge you to definitively disavow support from the various leaders and forms of white supremacist groups in the country. I plead with you to retract your order blocking Muslims from entering this country. I remind you that, as a Christian, affirming the uniqueness and irreplaceability of all human beings entails extending hospitality to the stranger, even if such hospitality entails risk.

Rather than a politics of divisiveness, please consider moving our country toward a politics of empathy where we are challenged to imagine what it would be like to be in the body of

- a woman who has been physically assaulted;
- a Muslim afraid to wear the hijab in public;
- those who are fearful of a hate crime because of their sexuality;
- individuals whose disability might subject them to mockery;
- people of color who live in a country where slavery is its original sin and who endure continual suspicion due to the color of their skin.

Such a politics of empathy is part of what Orthodox Christians would call a politics of *theosis*—it is part of our struggle to love as God loves in the world.

Dear President Trump, Vice President Pence, Members of the Trump Administration and the 115th Congress,

The story about Abraham bargaining with God to save the people of Sodom is well known, but the underpinning of this story is rarely recognized. After admonishing God, "Shall not the judge of all the earth deal justly?" (Genesis 18:25), Abraham does not suggest that God save only the righteous members of the city and destroy only its wicked inhabitants. Instead, Abraham tries to convince God to save the entire city due to the upright people within it. Abraham only gives up when God says that not even ten righteous individuals can be found there.

This text reflects a communitarian rather than an individualistic perspective. It embeds two complementary notions: that a small number of individuals can make change and thereby save an entire community, and that if decent individuals do not succeed in transforming their community, they are culpable.

> **Standing idly by, or arguing that someone else should step up, is not an option.**

In many ways this is a most un-American idea. After all, rugged individualism and self-reliance are core American values. But this biblical passage should make us more aware that as individuals—whether private citizens or public officials—we are each responsible for the members of the larger community and polity. Standing idly by, or arguing that someone else should step up, is not an option. We are each accountable if we do not work to improve our communities.

The prophet Ezekiel later refers to the story of Sodom when he lists the Sodomites' sins: "pride, excess of food, and prosperous ease." Then he adds that they "did not aid the poor and needy" (Ezekiel 16:49). Prosperity itself is not criticized. Instead, like the passage in Genesis, Ezekiel takes a communitarian perspective. The prophet insists that economic success requires obligations to the less fortunate: to the hungry, the poor, and the needy; other biblical texts add foreigners to that list. This is the role that each of us as private citizens must foster, and a role that each and every government official must advance.

Dear President Trump, Vice President Pence, Members of the Trump Administration and the 115th Congress,

"May grace and peace be yours" (1 Peter 1:2).

Every time this phrase occurs in the Bible, grace always comes before peace. There is no way to find peace unless grace comes first.

When peace eludes our hearts and anxiety reigns in our souls, grace is often the last place we turn. We try to talk our way out of fear and rationalize our way into peace. We separate ourselves from others to insulate ourselves from what we fear. But this is never successful in alleviating our fear. Only grace-filled love can cast out fear and lead us to peace.

Your administration begins its leadership at a time of great anxiety in our nation and our world. The fear of terrorism and economic insecurity results in suspicion of foreigners and those who are different from ourselves. Anxiety about the direction our country will take prompts painful divisions among neighbors, citizens, and families.

> *The only true balm to our national anxieties is abundant love . . .*

The Christian tradition teaches that only love can dispel the anxieties that plague us. If we try to rationalize our way out of these fears through argument or policy alone, we will never know peace. And no one finds real peace by building walls. The only true balm to our national anxieties is abundant love that stretches to citizens and immigrants, poor and rich, young and old, neighbors and strangers.

May your administration govern with a wisdom that is guided by love. May grace and peace be ours in abundance as a nation, so that we may be a beacon and a blessing to the world.

Karina Martin Hogan

Dear President Trump, Vice President Pence, Members of the Trump Administration and the 115th Congress,

The book of Ruth tells one of the most beloved tales of family loyalty in the Bible. But we sometimes overlook the fact that this biblical book also contains a story about immigrants and the sacrifices they make for their loved ones.

After Naomi and her two Moabite daughters-in-law, Ruth and Orpah, have been widowed, Naomi decides to leave her temporary residence in Moab and return to her hometown of Bethlehem in Judah. She urges her daughters-in-law to go back to their families, which Orpah does after some hesitation. But Ruth makes a different choice, telling Naomi: "Do not press me to leave you or to turn back from following you! Where you go, I will go. Where you lodge, I will lodge. Your people shall be my people, and your God my God" (Ruth 1:16).

Let's be as welcoming of the immigrants in our midst as the people of Bethlehem were to Ruth the Moabite, and later to the unwed mother of Jesus.

When Ruth leaves behind her family and her homeland, she also gives up her Moabite gods. The United States, however, has never demanded that its immigrants give up their religion. Many immigrants—including Muslims—still come to the United States for the sake of religious freedom.

After Ruth arrives in Bethlehem, she devises a plan to support herself and her mother-in-law by gleaning in the fields, a choice that involves backbreaking and risky labor for a young woman. Fortunately, she ends up in the field of Naomi's relative Boaz, who treats the vulnerable widow with kindness and generosity.

In the end, Ruth's sacrifices pay off: She marries Boaz and gives birth to Obed, the grandfather of King David. The Bible thus celebrates a foreign woman, an immigrant, as the matriarch of "the house and lineage of David" (Luke 2:4). The New Testament mentions Ruth by name as an ancestor of Jesus (Matthew 1:5).

Many immigrants to the United States not only leave their homelands and families, but they also sacrifice professional success and social status as they work in low-wage jobs for the sake of greater freedom and opportunity for their children. Let's be as welcoming of the immigrants in our midst as the people of Bethlehem were to Ruth the Moabite, and later to the unwed mother of Jesus.

Dear President Trump, Vice President Pence, Members of the Trump Administration and the 115th Congress,

As a Hindu American scholar, the sacred text that I think of at this time of political transition is the Bhagavad Gita and its call to work always for the universal common good (3:20 and 3:25). Consideration for the common good is what makes a person unselfish and wise and what should drive our public policy. After all, the state should exist for the promotion of the common good, not the interests of any particular group.

> " *Power without compassion is destructive . . .*

The Sanskrit word *lokasangraha*, which I translate here as "universal common good," is inclusive, encompassing human beings as well as the natural world. All are included because at the heart of my faith's teaching is the core claim that all beings embody equally the one divine being who is of ultimate value. This is the source of our reverence for all and the ground of our affirmation of human dignity and equal worth. Any laws we make or policies we formulate must affirm the equal worth, freedom, and dignity of all human beings regardless of race, sex, religion, or ancestry. We cannot compromise on this in words or actions.

In placing the universal common good at the center of our policymaking, we must devote ourselves in a special way to the well-being of those who suffer and those who are the victims of injustice. The implementation of policies that are just and that alleviate suffering must become the measure of our greatness as a nation. Power without compassion is destructive and becomes ethically and spiritually debilitating.

The Hindu poet Narsi Mehta reminds us to measure ourselves by our ability to feel the pain of others and act generously towards them. Likewise, Mahatma Gandhi taught compassion for those who suffer. I implore you to remember Gandhi's words whenever you struggle to make the right decision: "Recall the face of the poorest and weakest man [or woman] whom you have seen, and ask yourself if the step you contemplate is going to be of any use to him [or her]. Will he [or she] gain anything by it? . . . Then you will find your doubt and your self melting away."

Emilie M. Townes

Dear President Trump, Vice President Pence, Members of the Trump Administration and the 115th Congress,

The notion of the common good is one of the powerful public ideals that blends our civic and religious beliefs. The common good involves creating and maintaining social systems, institutions, and environments that we depend on to benefit all people. This form of justice is achieved through citizenship, collective action, and active participation in politics and public service—all sorts of strong religious and moral acts.

> *Governing our nation across difference to bring justice and healing to our world is exactly what we need from our elected officials.*

The idea of the common good originated over two thousand years ago in the writings of Plato, Aristotle, and Cicero. Centuries later, Pope Paul VI defined the common good as "the sum of those conditions of social life which allow social groups and their individual members relatively thorough and ready access to their own fulfillment" (*Gaudium et Spes*). The common good does not just happen. Establishing and maintaining the common good requires the cooperative efforts of citizens and their elected officials.

So, who will you be as you seek to serve the common good in the coming years? At the start of a new administration, we all should be guided by the powerful message in Hebrews 11:1: "Now faith is the substance of things hoped for, the evidence of things not seen." We should keep this verse in mind as we blend faith in our country and its many people with the need to pull ourselves toward a common good—a common good that is neither selective nor narrow, but instead points us to a sense of welcoming one another into each other's lives.

In *Just Hospitality: God's Welcome in a World of Difference*, Letty M. Russell writes: "Hospitality is the practice of God's welcome by reaching across difference to participate in God's actions bringing justice and healing to our world in crisis." Governing our nation across difference to bring justice and healing to our world is exactly what we need from our elected officials. This is precisely how we can bring about "things hoped for."

Please focus on the common good for our nation—all of it, all of us—as you govern.

Carmen Nanko-Fernández

Dear President Trump, Vice President Pence, Members of the Trump Administration and the 115th Congress,

On the National Mall in the Hirshhorn Sculpture Garden stands *El Profeta*, sculpted in the 1930s by Spanish artist Pablo Gargallo. This prophet resembles those unnerving figures throughout human history and across religious traditions who make us profoundly uncomfortable with their exhortations and calls for accountability.

With mouth wide open and hand upraised, in this prophet's presence we feel the thunderous roar for justice, hear the cries that disturb our peace: the wail of parents who lose their kids to violence, the rage of laborers demanding their fair and due wage, the shouts of teachers for the resources they need for their underserved kids, and students begging for relief from onerous lifelong debt.

The frailness of the prophet's body belies the strength possessed in the vulnerable frame, a hint of the power of those too often underestimated or dismissed because of age, illness, disability, poverty. From the depths of these bodies emanates expectations of health care, access, and equal protections under the law for all, because in honoring these claims on society we are all cared for, we are all protected.

This prophet resembles those unnerving figures . . . who make us profoundly uncomfortable with their exhortations and calls for accountability.

The most distinctive features of *El Profeta* are its disproportionately large feet, reminding us that prophets speak truth rooted in commitments to real communities. Prophets are planted firmly as guardians of the land, seekers of the heavens, protectors of water. They work the earth: farmers, miners, migrant laborers, environmental activists. They are embedded in place: the young DREAMers, the grandparents of Selma, those who insist that Black Lives Matter, that immigrants are not illegal, and that alt-white is not all right. They honor the country they love and seek the peace, some through their military or public service, and others through the risky business of conscientious objection and social protest. These prophets are at home in cyberspace, on social media, in our streets, our schools, our houses of worship, our barrios. They are rooted and invested in the well-being of this nation.

Gargallo's *Profeta* summons us to heed our obligations to each other, to navigate the tensions of building a just society, and to resist everything that demeans the dignity of life and creation.

Dear President Trump, Vice President Pence, Members of the Trump Administration and the 115th Congress,

> "
>
> *Political offices, even as they bring honor and power, demand humility and commitment to "doing what is right and good."*

The biblical book of Deuteronomy lays out a vision of leadership in its laws of the king. Alongside limiting his extravagance, the king must keep a copy of the law with him and "read it all his life so that he may learn to revere his God . . . [and] not act haughtily towards his fellows" (Deuteronomy 17:18–20). The law's express purpose is to teach the king humility. The king and his subjects are "fellows," literally "brothers." No one, not even the most powerful human authority, is above the law.

Consonant with this legislative vision, the biblical prophets regularly call kings to task for abusing the power of their office. Thus, Jeremiah stands in the ostentatious residence of the Judean king Jehoiakim and excoriates the injustice his palace represents (Jeremiah 22:13–15):

> Woe to him who builds his house without righteousness
> and his upper rooms without justice,
> Who makes his fellow work for nothing,
> his wages he does not give him,
> Who says: "I will build for myself a vast palace
> with spacious upper rooms,"
> And who frames for himself windows,
> paneled in cedar, painted with vermilion.
> Are you a king because you compete in cedar?

The prophet peels away the royal red paint and wood paneling to expose the palace's weak foundation. Built on the backs of poorly paid workers, the building—beautiful though it may be—undermines the ideals of justice the king is meant to uphold.

There are obvious differences between kingship in ancient Israel and the modern American presidency. Nevertheless, this aspect of the Bible's message remains relevant to our leaders today. Political offices, even as they bring honor and power, demand humility and commitment to "doing what is right and good" (Deuteronomy 6:18).

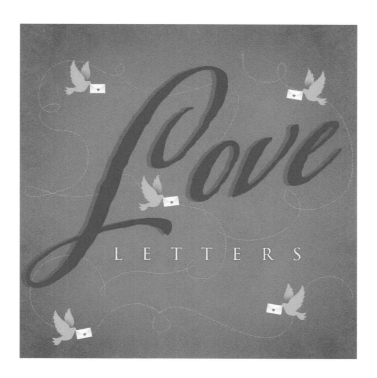

We designed graphics like this to link holidays that occurred during the 100 days to relevant letters. The four letters published on and around Valentine's Day on February 14, 2017 (Letters 24–27) all mention love, including Letter 26 by Tamara Eskenazi, who teaches: "To love others is to take responsibility for their well-being."

RELIGIOUS VOICES: DAY 21–30

LETTER 21 | FEBRUARY 9, 2017

Katharine R. Henderson

President, Auburn Seminary

LETTER 26 | FEBRUARY 14, 2017

Tamara Cohn Eskenazi

The Effie Wise Ochs Professor of Biblical Literature and History, Hebrew Union College–Jewish Institute of Religion, Los Angeles

LETTER 22 | FEBRUARY 10, 2017

Corrine Carvalho

Professor of Theology & Interim Dean of Social Work, University of St. Thomas

LETTER 27 | FEBRUARY 15, 2017

Karen L. King

Hollis Professor of Divinity, Harvard University

LETTER 23 | FEBRUARY 11, 2017

Margaret Aymer

First Presbyterian Church, Shreveport, D. Thomason Professor of New Testament, Austin Presbyterian Theological Seminary

LETTER 28 | FEBRUARY 16, 2017

Mark S. Smith

Helena Professor of Old Testament Literature and Exegesis, Princeton Theological Seminary

LETTER 24 | FEBRUARY 12, 2017

Bryan N. Massingale

Professor of Theological and Social Ethics, Fordham University

LETTER 29 | FEBRUARY 17, 2017

Emran El-Badawi

Program Director & Associate Professor of Middle Eastern Studies, University of Houston

LETTER 25 | FEBRUARY 13, 2017

Simran Jeet Singh

Post-Doctoral Fellow, New York University Center for Religion and Media

LETTER 30 | FEBRUARY 18, 2017

Joshua D. Garroway

Associate Professor of Early Christianity and Second Commonwealth Judaism, Hebrew Union College–Jewish Institute of Religion, Los Angeles

Dear President Trump, Vice President Pence, Members of the Trump Administration and the 115th Congress,

I am president of Auburn Seminary, a 200-year-old institution founded by Presbyterians in upstate New York to train leaders "hardy" enough for the frontier. Leadership is my business, and, as you know, what makes for success in one time may not work in the next. Becoming president marks a new time for your leadership, and America needs you to be the best president you can be.

The winning formula for leadership (or life, for that matter) in our tradition comes from a passage in the book of Ephesians that talks about putting on the "whole armor of God" (Ephesians 6:10–17). You might think that this means being strong, powerful, wealthy, and secure in the usual sense. But, here is what "suiting up" in this context actually means: put on the "belt of truth," which means be truthful based on the best facts and evidence available. Then, put on the "breastplate of righteousness," which means lead a life that pursues justice and therefore is pleasing to God. For your shoes, put on whatever inspires you to walk in the way of peace and love, not war and violence. Finally, "take the shield of faith" and "the helmet of salvation" and pray for *all* the people, as Scripture says: "Peace be to the whole community, and love with faith" (6:23).

> "
> *. . . put on the "belt of truth," which means be truthful based on the best facts and evidence available.*

President Trump, I pray that you will heed these words at this new moment of leadership. The values you invoked at the end of your inauguration speech—power, security, pride, and wealth—are not God's values; and they will not make America great. Instead, put on the whole armor of God: Seek truth, do justice, walk humbly, offer hope. Open your heart and mind to many voices, especially those who disagree with you. Use your power well so that you might do great things for all God's creatures—including women, Muslims, and immigrants—all those made in God's image who yearn for an equal place at America's table.

Pray sincerely for all the people, and know I will be praying for you.

Dear President Trump, Vice President Pence, Members of the Trump Administration and the 115th Congress,

I write to you as a biblical scholar who knows how much the Bible has influenced American culture. I invite you—elected representatives of our nation who are charged to enact the values embedded in the Constitution, values with roots in biblical traditions—to reflect on the complexity of that charge.

> **The king's blind self-confidence puts the national security of the entire land at risk.**

I think about the state of our nation through the lens of the prophetic texts that continue to speak honestly about our flawed human condition. The book of Jeremiah, in particular, reflects the tragic consequences of foolish leaders who refuse to heed the warnings of national disaster.

Throughout the book, Jeremiah predicts that Jerusalem will fall to the Babylonian assault, repeatedly describing the dire fate that becomes a reality in 587 BCE. Although the book often casts the whole nation as sinful, Jeremiah's interactions with those in power make it clear that the citizens of the city suffer because of the decisions of their trusted leaders.

In chapter 36, King Jehoiakim burns a scroll that contains Jeremiah's pronouncements, thinking that he thereby will silence the critical and disruptive prophet. Especially given the infrequency of written texts at that time, the king's action amounts to state-sponsored censorship, a desperate attempt to change history and alter the nation's fate. But the city's destruction demonstrates the king's folly.

As your presidency begins, the nation watches to see what kind of leader you will be. When Jehoiakim burns the scroll, he feels none of the trepidation or uncertainty experienced by many of his advisors. The king's blind self-confidence puts the national security of the entire land at risk. Will the confidence of our elected leaders reach to that level of hubris and folly? Will you be able to discern the wise and prescient voices among the cacophony of advice you receive?

I hope and pray that the next four years turn out to be a beacon in American history, a time that ushers in a new era of humble servant-leaders who can listen to wise counsel. The fate of the nation rests with you.

DAY 23, LETTER 23 *Margaret Aymer*

Dear President Trump, Vice President Pence, Members of the Trump Administration and the 115th Congress,

As Americans, we often confuse power and importance. Some even think our society's powerful people necessarily speak with divine authority. The Gospel of Luke warns us against such hubris.

At the opening of chapter 3, Luke writes about rulers of great importance, like Pontius Pilate who governed Judea, Herod who ruled the Galilee, and Annas and Caiaphas who presided in the Jerusalem Temple. Did God speak to these great men, surrounded by their counselors, wealth, status, and military might? No, instead, God's word came to John in the wilderness, an unknown Galilean peasant baptizing people in the river. He was a backwater man from a backwater place, someone who might even have been considered a "loser." Yet God singled out John the Baptist, rather than any of those perceived as powerful in Roman or Judean society.

Through John the Baptist, God spoke a warning and a call. John warned that one's ancestry does not assure one's righteousness before God (Luke 3:7–8). John called for redistributive justice: sharing one's wealth with the poor. He taught: "Whoever has two coats must share with anyone who has none; and whoever has food, must do likewise" (3:11). John also condemned unjust business practices: "Do not extort money from anyone by threats or false accusation" (3:14).

> **As Americans, we often confuse power and importance.**

As you begin your service to the people of the United States of America, heed well the Gospel of Luke. Do not be swayed by those who would elevate any powerful person's word to divine status. Instead, attend to those whom some in our society might call "losers": the black, the brown, the immigrant and the poor, women and children, those without status or money or power. After all, Luke testifies that God's word may well come to the United States through their witness.

Dear President Trump, Vice President Pence, Members of the Trump Administration and the 115th Congress,

I write this letter as the Trump presidency unfolds, with a sense of dread about our nation's future. This anxiety stems not solely from disagreements with proposed policies, but from what this election has revealed about who we are as a nation. The election showed that we are not only deeply divided by fissures of race, class, gender, ethnicity, geography, religion, and sexual identities and expressions; we also are separated by chasms of understanding. Those who differ from us seem increasingly alien and incomprehensible. We have become a nation of strangers, siloed in racial, geographic, media, and even digital enclaves where we mostly interact with those who are like us.

Isolation fuels ignorance, indifference, and fear. These become fertile soil for moral callousness: a cold disregard for those not like us, evidenced in the vitriol of our public discourse and a spike in hate crimes. This callousness and even cruelty toward those not like us fills me with dread.

The sacred texts of Christianity summon us to love our neighbor, care for the stranger, and show one another the compassion we believe God has for us (Luke 6:36; 10:25–37). They bluntly tell us that we are our brother's and sister's keeper (Genesis 4:9). They warn us that our response to the least among us—those not like us—is the measure of our holiness and righteousness (Matthew 25:31–46).

> *Healing our divisions will come only from a cultivation of public compassion...*

Healing our national estrangement, then, is perhaps the greatest challenge facing your presidency. As Abraham Lincoln warned in his 1858 speech to the Illinois Republican State Convention: "A house divided against itself cannot stand."

But this healing will not come from facile appeals to unity, and even less from a dismissive attitude of "we won, get over it." Healing our divisions will come only from a cultivation of public compassion, which at the very least demands respect and decency toward those with whom we disagree.

Pope John Paul II declared that one of the most important questions facing a society is: "How are we living together?" *Together.* Mr. Trump, our collective response to that question will depend greatly upon both your compassion for the vulnerable and the quality of your respect for those with whom you disagree.

Dear President Trump, Vice President Pence, Members of the Trump Administration and the 115th Congress,

Let me open by stating that I respect each of you. My Sikh faith teaches me that the Divine created us all and resides within each of us.

However, while I honor your inherent divinity, I question your humanity. What does it mean for me as a Sikh to face a president who gained power by dehumanizing others and acting inhumanely? What does it mean for all people of faith to watch leaders in the White House who, on the campaign trail and now in office, contribute to immense social fracturing and fuel flames of bigotry and hate across the United States? Our nation has witnessed an incredible increase in hate incidents since you came to power. As a Sikh man with a turban and beard, I have experienced this rise in racism and violence firsthand. My community is under attack, as are many others in this country.

As a Sikh, I reject as unacceptable the xenophobia and intolerance you have engendered. When Babur entered South Asia and massacred innocent civilians, Guru Nanak, the founder of Sikhism, opposed him openly and fearlessly. He declared that anyone in power who attacks the disenfranchised would be held accountable. He stood firmly against injustice. His commitment to doing the right thing and to equal rights is at the foundation of the Sikh belief system. This is a universal ethic to which all humanity can subscribe.

> **The Sikh model of justice is rooted in love.**

The Sikh model of justice is rooted in love. As a result, I seek not to espouse hatred, but to oppose the injustices that you have incited and to explain why, as a Sikh, I cannot stand by idly while various religious and ethnic groups around our country are attacked and marginalized. Please know that Sikhs and Americans of good conscience across the land will continue to oppose you—fearlessly and unapologetically—until and unless you treat all people with the dignity and respect they deserve.

Dear President Trump, Vice President Pence, Members of the Trump Administration and the 115th Congress,

The Bible has been a major force in the formation of this country and the shaping of its religious values. In the Torah (or Pentateuch), the foundational part of the Bible shared by Jews and Christians, we find a commandment that has come to be regarded as the "Golden Rule": "Love your neighbor as yourself" (Leviticus 19:18).

Love in the Bible is about commitment, loyalty, and action, rather than feelings. To love others is to take responsibility for their well-being.

A less famous, but even more extraordinary biblical verse commands: "You shall love the *stranger* as yourself"! The larger passage states: "When a stranger [Hebrew *ger*, or 'resident alien'] resides with you in your land, you shall not oppress the stranger. The stranger who resides with you shall be to you as the citizen among you; you shall love the stranger as yourself, for you were strangers in the land of Egypt: I am the Lord your God" (Leviticus 19:33–34).

> **Love in the Bible is about commitment, loyalty, and action, rather than feelings.**

Laws in the Jewish scriptures repeatedly insist that minority groups be accorded rights and legal protection (for example, Numbers 15:16) and share the blessings that accrue: "You shall rejoice in your festival, with your son and daughter, your male and female slave, the Levite, the stranger, the fatherless, and the widow in your communities" (Deuteronomy 16:14).

The biblical prophets likewise underscore the significance of caring for the disenfranchised, warning that a society is only as strong as its most vulnerable members. Prophets rightly note that greed and gross inequality destroy the very foundations of society and bring about the collapse of the entire nation. Do not think, declares the prophet Jeremiah, that you can exploit others and consider yourselves safe (Jeremiah 7:1–15).

These core biblical teachings have not lost their relevance for our time. Given all that America is and can be, these ancient words call out to us even more urgently today.

Dear President Trump, Vice President Pence, Members of the Trump Administration and the 115th Congress,

In these complex times, the tasks before you, and before all of us, are difficult. I have spent a lot of time thinking about Jesus' Sermon on the Mount (Matthew 5:38–48), where he tells us to be perfect as our heavenly Father is perfect. What does this mean?

Jesus instructs us not to resist an evildoer. If anyone strikes us on the right cheek, he says, turn the other cheek. If someone sues you for your coat, give away your shirt too. If you are forced to carry a person's burden for one mile, go for two. Give to anyone who asks, Jesus teaches. Really? All of this can and has been dismissed as naive and impractical, if not downright caving in to injustice and violent force. But it gets worse: "Love your enemies and pray for those who persecute you," Jesus instructs. Okay, but only from a position of power, right? No, Jesus explains that we should act this way in order to be like God. God sends the shining sun and the nourishing rain to everyone, without consideration. Be perfect, Jesus insists. Be like God.

To do that, we can't always see ourselves, our group, or our country as the righteous victims. Aren't we also the ones who desire to dominate others, who try to possess as much as we can get, who act violently? Aren't we the ones who seek revenge on our enemies?

> *God sends the shining sun and the nourishing rain to everyone, without consideration.*

I've come to believe that when we cultivate Jesus' point of view, we actually start to see things more clearly. When we act out of love and generosity, we start to defeat the worst impulses of our fallen nature. Instead of meeting despair with violence, pain with hatred, humiliation with vengeance, fear with the false security of feeble fences and fake news, we can lend mutual support for effective problem-solving and for building sustained peace and prosperity. We can feel deeply grateful for the shining sun and nourishing rain.

Jesus' advice is not impractical. It is precisely what might save us.

Dear President Trump, Vice President Pence, Members of the Trump Administration and the 115th Congress,

For centuries, America has enjoyed a powerful vision of a great people and society bound together. Yet today our country faces a lack of confidence in our American vision, largely because we have forgotten that, as we recite in the Pledge of Allegiance, we are joined as "one nation under God, indivisible, with liberty and justice for all."

Many of us take pride in how our American vision goes back to the covenant of the Bible. We find the essence of the Bible's own vision of being "one nation under God" beautifully expressed by the prophet Malachi when he asks Israel about its actions in trying times (2:10):

> Do we all not have one parent?
> Did not one God create us?
> Why then does each of us deal treacherously with one another,
> Desecrating the covenant of our ancestors?

The prophet reminds us that we all share the same divine parent: the one God of Israel and the world who bestows upon us our God-given dignity. We are all linked together by our shared humanity, which comes from being created by this one parent-god.

> *. . . we are all bound together in God's covenant, a sacred relationship that involves mutual responsibilities and expectations.*

What's more, the prophet tells us that we are all bound together in God's covenant, a sacred relationship that involves mutual responsibilities and expectations. We are asked to make this covenant-relationship real through kind and generous dealings with one another day in and day out. If we care about America, we need to care about each other; we need to respect and help one another. If we care about America, we need to care about justice for all.

The Bible warns us: "Where there is no vision, the people perish" (Proverbs 29:18). Mr. President, what really is your vision for America? How will you fulfill your pledge to serve our "one nation under God, indivisible, with liberty and justice for all"?

Dear President Trump, Vice President Pence, Members of the Trump Administration and the 115th Congress,

America's native son, James Baldwin, warned us that to describe people as terrorists "is to dismiss their claim to human attention: we are not compelled to think of them at all anymore, except as the vermin that must be destroyed" (*The Evidence of Things Not Seen*). Your policies against Muslim immigrants and refugees under the pretext of terrorism reopen a dark page in our nation's history.

America was founded as a nation of immigrants, and Muslims have been part of the American story since the very beginning. Millions of Muslims were among the African slaves who suffered grave injustice and built this nation on their backs. George Washington's letter to his "great and magnanimous friend" Sultan Muhammad Ibn Abdullah of Morocco and Thomas Jefferson's Qur'an show that America's Founding Fathers recognized Islam's importance for international diplomacy and personal philosophy.

Some two centuries later, however, our current leaders have alienated, even dehumanized, their fellow Muslim citizens, with episodes of racism on the rise on your watch.

Scripture teaches us that long ago, different peoples settled in the land of Egypt as they searched for economic opportunity and an honorable life. Like America, Egypt was once a great nation of immigrants and natives, slaves and masters. Its ruler, Pharaoh, was considered a god: a narcissist and a dictator of the masses. When a young foreign slave named Joseph arrived in Egypt, the Qur'an teaches that his master commanded, "Make his stay honorable. He may well be of use to us, or we may adopt him as a son. And thus We settled Joseph in that land" (12:21).

> " *America is fundamentally a nation of immigrants . . . who go on to do great things for their adopted nation.*

America is fundamentally a nation of immigrants, a home blessed with honorable sons and daughters, like Joseph, who go on to do great things for their adopted nation. The future of America depends in large part on how your administration treats its Muslim citizens, residents and immigrants alike. Leaders come and go; but diversity and pluralism are here to stay. Like the ancients awaiting a sign from the heavens, we the people endure. We take heart in the words of the Qur'an: "Be witnesses of justice, and let not the hatred of a people prevent you from being just" (5:8).

Dear President Trump, Vice President Pence, Members of the Trump Administration and the 115th Congress,

> *. . . Moses instructs the Israelites with exhausting frequency to show special kindness to the most vulnerable members of society . . .*

Our founders regarded the American Revolution as a reenactment of the biblical Exodus. Divine Providence, they figured, rescued the colonists from England, just as God had saved the Israelites from Egyptian bondage. Not surprisingly, Benjamin Franklin and Thomas Jefferson recommended that our nation's Great Seal be emblazoned with imagery from the Exodus.

While comparisons between America and ancient Israel tend to focus on times of triumph, we should not overlook more tragic moments. Right after their salvation, the Israelites endured adversity. As the throng pressed forward, wearied and frightened by the wilderness, some Israelites struggled to keep up. The aged and infirm were abandoned in the rear, defenseless when Amalek and his men attacked from behind (Deuteronomy 25:18). The Israelites circled back to vanquish the Amalekites, but the initial losses they incurred had a lasting impact on the Israelite consciousness: Never again should weariness or fear lead Israel to neglect its most vulnerable constituents. To stress that message, Moses instructs the Israelites with exhausting frequency to show special kindness to the most vulnerable members of society: to widows, orphans, strangers, and the poor (Deuteronomy 10:18; 14:29; 16:11; 24:19; 26:12; 27:19).

Like the Israelites, we Americans have at times let fear obscure our lofty ideals. Tomorrow marks 75 years since President Franklin D. Roosevelt signed Executive Order 9066 on February 19, 1942, which sent tens of thousands of Japanese American citizens to internment camps. I live close to the Santa Anita racetrack, which was one of the assembly centers for the internment. It stands today as a beautiful venue, but also an enduring reminder of a time when we, the people, regrettably abandoned our responsibility to secure the blessings of liberty and justice for all who dwell in our midst.

In this present moment of anxiety, when the fear of terror might move us to neglect our historic embrace of those who are vulnerable and seeking shelter, our nation needs prophetic leadership. At a time when so many Americans feel apprehensive about health care, education, and the prospects for a brighter tomorrow, we need leaders who, like Moses, will insist upon the compassionate treatment of the stranger and the poor, even in the face of fear.

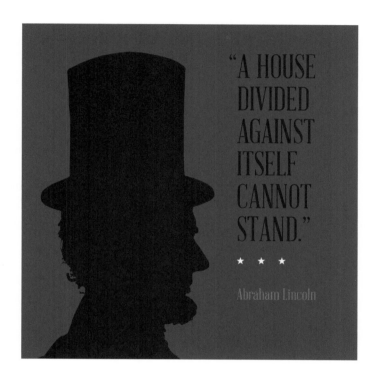

Letter 24 by Bryan Massingale, which appeared on Lincoln's Birthday, quotes President Lincoln's "house divided" speech. The five letters surrounding Presidents' Day on February 20, 2017 (Letters 29–33) all mention past U.S. presidents.

RELIGIOUS VOICES: DAY 31–40

LETTER 31 | FEBRUARY 19, 2017

Yii-Jan Lin

Assistant Professor of New Testament,
Yale Divinity School

LETTER 32 | FEBRUARY 20, 2017

Tat-siong Benny Liew

Class of 1956 Professor in New Testament
Studies, College of the Holy Cross

LETTER 33 | FEBRUARY 21, 2017

Amy-Jill Levine

University Professor of New Testament
and Jewish Studies, Vanderbilt
University Divinity School & College of
Arts and Science

LETTER 34 | FEBRUARY 22, 2017

Jacqueline M. Hidalgo

Associate Professor of Latina/o Studies
and Religion, Williams College

LETTER 35 | FEBRUARY 23, 2017

Paul W. Chilcote

Professor of Historical Theology and
Wesleyan Studies, Asbury Theological
Seminary

LETTER 36 | FEBRUARY 24, 2017

Murali Balaji

Founder, Maruthi Education Consulting
& Lecturer, Annenberg School for
Communications, University of
Pennsylvania

LETTER 37 | FEBRUARY 25, 2017

Danielle Widmann Abraham

Assistant Professor of Comparative
Religion and Islamic Studies,
Ursinus College

LETTER 38 | FEBRUARY 26, 2017

Althea Spencer Miller

Assistant Professor of New Testament,
Drew Theological School

LETTER 39 | FEBRUARY 27, 2017

William P. Brown

William Marcellus McPheeters Professor
of Old Testament, Columbia Theological
Seminary

LETTER 40 | FEBRUARY 28, 2017

Randy S. Woodley

Distinguished Professor of Faith and
Culture & Director of Intercultural
and Indigenous Studies, George Fox
University and Portland Seminary

Dear President Trump, Vice President Pence, Members of the Trump Administration and the 115th Congress,

In his farewell speech to the nation in 1989, President Ronald Reagan spoke of his vision for America, describing the country as a "shining city . . . with free ports that hummed with commerce and creativity, and if there had to be city walls, the walls had doors and the doors were open to anyone with the will and the heart to get here."

Anyone in the audience schooled in the Bible would have known that President Reagan was invoking imagery from the New Testament, the book of Revelation in particular. Revelation 21 presents the New Jerusalem, the ultimate utopian city, full of power—"the kings of the earth will bring their glory into it" (v. 24)—and wealth—"the city is pure gold" (v. 18). There *are* walls and gates, but the gates are *never* shut, so that people of every kind can "bring into it the glory and the honor of the nations" (v. 26). This New Jerusalem was inspired in part by Rome, an empire that, despite its cruelty, disregarded boundaries and differences of religion in citizenship for the sake of its enduring glory.

Mr. President, I do not believe in walls and gates. I do not need a city of gold. I prefer Jesus' boundary-less wandering and good news for the poor, sick, and forgotten. However, if you want America to represent power and wealth, look no further than Revelation and Ronald Reagan—the iconic Republican president of the last century—for a fantastic vision of glory and fame with open gates and doors. Both the writer of Revelation and Reagan knew that inviting others in and playing host to the nations of the earth meant greater wealth and power, not less.

> " *. . . look no further than Revelation and Ronald Reagan for a fantastic vision of glory and fame with open gates and doors.*

Dear President Trump, Vice President Pence, Members of the Trump Administration and the 115th Congress,

"Every gun that is made, every warship launched, every rocket fired signifies, in the final sense, a theft from those who hunger and are not fed, those who are cold and are not clothed."

These are the words of Dwight D. Eisenhower, the thirty-fourth president of our country and a five-star general of the army. President Eisenhower's words echo the message of the well-known parable about Jesus separating the sheep (the just) and the goats (the unjust), which in some Bibles carries the caption, "The Judgment of the Nations" (Matthew 25:31–46). Jesus makes it clear that what really counts is not whether we become his followers and call him "Lord," but how we act in the world—especially how we treat those who are vulnerable and in need: those who are hungry, thirsty, foreign, naked, sick, or jailed.

This message makes sense since, according to Matthew, Jesus himself was among "the least of these" (25:40). Jesus was welcomed by people of another land, ethnicity, and religion at his birth (the Zoroastrian magi in 2:1–12); and he became a migrant or refugee to Egypt as a toddler because of political oppression by Herod (2:13–18). As a colonized Jewish person within the mighty Roman Empire, Jesus certainly knew the painful realities of living life and facing death (Matthew 27).

> *We need more laws and institutions in our nation that aim to actualize Matthew's message and protect the vulnerable.*

We find a similar concern for "the least of these," regardless of their origin or religious affiliation, on the pedestal of the Statue of Liberty: "Give me your tired, your poor, your huddled masses yearning to breathe free." We need more laws and institutions in our nation that aim to actualize Matthew's message and protect the vulnerable.

Several presidents from both major parties—including Presidents Coolidge, Kennedy, and Obama—have cited or alluded to another core teaching from Matthew's Gospel, Jesus' "Golden Rule": "In everything do to others as you would have them do to you" (7:12).

These verses from Matthew show, however, that our actions often lag behind our rhetoric. I pray that our country under your administration will live out and live up to what we say we value as followers of Christ or as people of the United States of America.

Dear President Trump, Vice President Pence, Members of the Trump Administration and the 115th Congress,

In his 2001 inaugural address, George W. Bush said: "I can pledge our nation to a goal: When we see that wounded traveler on the road to Jericho, we will not pass to the other side." President Bush was alluding to the parable of the good Samaritan (Luke 10:25–37), and he casts America as the generous Samaritan. The parable is much more provocative.

In the run-up to the parable, a lawyer quotes Leviticus 19:18, "You shall love your neighbor as yourself," and then he asks Jesus, "Who is my neighbor?" This is, legally speaking, a good question. Neighbors have rights and responsibilities that aliens lack. In biblical terms, Canadians and Mexicans are not "neighbors," but "aliens." Yet when it comes to love, the distinction is irrelevant. Leviticus 19:34 mandates: "The alien who resides with you shall be to you as the citizen among you; you shall love the alien as yourself, for you were aliens in the land of Egypt."

> " *. . . those whom we call enemies may, in fact, be our rescuers.*

For Jesus, distinguishing neighbors from aliens is not the pressing question. He recounts how robbers attacked a man on the Jerusalem-to-Jericho road and left him for dead. Two neighbors, a priest and a Levite, who should have stopped to help, pass him by. But a Samaritan displays compassion: tending the victim's wounds, bringing him to Jericho, entrusting him to an innkeeper's care. With the Samaritan, the story moves from neighbor not simply to alien, but to enemy.

President Bush identified America with the Samaritan, but that is not how Jesus' original Jewish audience would have heard the parable. At the time, Jews and Samaritans generally hated each other. The idea of a Samaritan showing compassion to a Jew was almost unthinkable.

The lawyer asks, "Who is my neighbor?" but Jesus poses the better question, "Which of these three was a neighbor?" The lawyer can't bring himself to say "Samaritan," but he correctly answers: "The one who showed him mercy." Jesus replies, "Go and do likewise."

Mercy must be shown not only to neighbors and not only to aliens, but even to enemies. Harder still, we must recognize that those whom we call enemies may, in fact, be our rescuers. We are all created in the divine image (Genesis 1:26–27). To forget that connection deprives us of our humanity.

Dear President Trump, Vice President Pence, Members of the Trump Administration and the 115th Congress,

When invited to join this impressive array of scholars writing to you these first 100 days, I agreed because I had faith that centuries of Latina and Catholic thought would offer up common hope about a future we somehow must build together. Despite the wealth of these traditions, I struggled to write this letter.

President Trump, you once publicly cited 2 Corinthians, a collection of letters that affirm the necessity and virtue of hope. In 2 Corinthians 1:7, Paul writes of a communal hope that stands firm because we know we are companions who share in the same sufferings and the same consolation. But can there be hope if you do not, like Paul, view all those around you as "brothers and sisters" with shared sufferings and shared consolation? Can there be hope if speeches and tweets malign communities and individuals, especially the U.S. communities to which I belong as a Latina, a woman, and a scholar? With all that has been said and done, I must ask, do we share in either our sufferings or our consolation? I worry that this country, indeed the species of homo sapiens, is as divided as we seem. I worry that we may never become a "more perfect union."

> *I . . . remain determined to build—and we will build—a more racially, culturally, and economically just United States of America.*

In December, I saw Theater Mitu's performance of the play *Juárez: A Documentary Mythology*. The play wrestles with the tragedy of mass murder, particularly the targeting of young indigenous and mixed-race women in the border city of Juárez, Mexico. Among the voices quoted in the play is an activist fighting for justice for the thousands of people gruesomely murdered. He observes that Juárez's situation is too dire for hope. In times like this, he claims, all we have is determination. "It's sad, and it's difficult," says one person in the play. Another asserts: "The bad is not over. The good is not over."

Although hope that we might bridge the divisions evades me now, I write with the conviction that millions, including myself, remain determined to build—and we will build—a more racially, culturally, and economically just United States of America.

Paul W. Chilcote

Dear President Trump, Vice President Pence, Members of the Trump Administration and the 115th Congress,

Spiritual character defines us as human beings. The practice of virtues shapes communities, even nations, with hospitality standing out as one of the virtues that has become increasingly important in my life of faith. The shape of my own family—now representing four continents—reflects this virtue. Hospitality made this gift of love possible.

> "
>
> *An administration characterized by hospitality will sow seeds of hope, the implications of which are boundless . . .*

You may not recognize the name Jürgen Moltmann. He is a German theologian known as the father of the "theology of hope." He once told me a story about his experience in World War II that shaped my life.

During the war there was a German prisoner of war camp in England. A young pastor and his wife served a small Methodist circuit of churches in the neighborhood. They were filled with compassion for the soldiers there and spurred to action. So they went to the commander and asked permission to take a prisoner with them to church each Sunday, and then to their home where they would share a meal. Surprisingly, the commander agreed. Sunday after Sunday, a steady flow of German soldiers worshiped and ate with the pastor and his wife in their home. This world-famous theologian looked at me intently and said, "One of those soldiers was a young man by the name of Jürgen Moltmann. And I want you to know that the seed of hope was planted in my heart around Frank and Nellie Baker's dinner table."

I encourage you to practice this virtue of hospitality and weave it into the life of your administration. I believe all people today yearn for hope. An administration characterized by hospitality will sow seeds of hope, the implications of which are boundless, shaping immigration policy, relations with enemies and allies alike, and the way we look at people different from ourselves. I pray that our nation will be a table of hospitality that makes the gift of love possible.

Dear President Trump, Vice President Pence, Members of the Trump Administration and the 115th Congress,

Over the last few months, I have wondered what it means to have a divided country in which people are no longer willing to see themselves in others. We seem to be in a dark period where polarization, distrust, and animosity prevent us from progress towards a more perfect union.

We continue to fight poverty, economic and social inequality, xenophobia, climate change, and a growing absence of empathy. All of these are daunting challenges at this particular moment in our history.

The question I ask is: "What can we do to create light together?"

> **What can we do to create light together?**

Hindu scriptures are replete with stories and prayers that affirm that good and light always prevail, even if it takes more than one lifetime (or many). That is why Hindu philosophy is predicated upon the idea that our universe exists in cycles. That is why we must never fall into the complacency of believing that our job in striving for good is complete.

For many Hindus, the *Ramayana* is the ultimate allegory of going through darkness to return to the light. In this ancient Sanskrit epic, Lord Rama returns from exile after defeating King Ravana (the metaphorical triumph of good over evil), with villagers celebrating his victory by lighting lamps.

As we navigate through turbulence, we must remember that our society can emerge stronger out of the darkness. We must recognize that we are in this together, and that the betterment of all requires more than safeguarding our own self-interests. I am strengthened by my faith's eternal optimism that our spiritual journey is ongoing, as is our work bettering American democracy together.

I conclude this letter with the *Pavamana Mantra*, which embodies our desire for truth and light.

asato mā sad gamaya,
tamaso mā jyotir gamaya,
mṛtyor māmṛtaṃ gamaya

Lead me from falsehood to truth,
Lead me from darkness to light,
Lead me from death to immortality.

Dear President Trump, Vice President Pence, Members of the Trump Administration and the 115th Congress,

Our country today faces a choice: Will we be a nation of values, or a nation of power for power's sake? In making this choice, my Quaker tradition teaches that we are anchored first and foremost in one truth: Because God created humankind "in His own image" (Genesis 1:27), every person in this world has within them the Light of God. Divinity is present in each human life.

Our country has brought together human lives from around the world: those from the first nations of this land, those whose ancestors resiliently survived being brought here by force, those who wanted freedom to worship or a better life for their children, and those who have come here to find a refuge when their lives were almost destroyed. With our distinct histories, we are now a people bound together. Recognizing this gives us strength.

John Woolman, an eighteenth-century Quaker preacher and abolitionist, asserted: "To consider mankind other than brethren . . . plainly supposes a darkness of understanding." We cannot afford to let xenophobia rob us of our place in the human family. We cannot afford to let bigotry subject us to that darkness. We must fight against anything that jeopardizes our ability to see one another as essential to our kindred reality.

> *What matters is that we nurture the life, the light, and the minds of our people.*

Our universe of obligation is marked first by the borders of our nation and then extends to the limits of our planet. We need the clearest possible vision to help us focus on improving the well-being of the people in our country and around the world. Today, one in five children in the United States lives in poverty. It is our task to ensure for them and for all children a life that is nourished, safe, secure, sustainable, and healthy.

We are commanded to care for each other and the strangers who come to our door. Winning for the sake of winning and power for the sake of domination and division mean nothing. What matters is that we nurture the life, the light, and the minds of our people. This culture of care is and will always be our peace.

As you go forward, I hold you and all of us in the Light.

Dear President Trump, Vice President Pence, Members of the Trump Administration and the 115th Congress,

The notion of covenant is fundamental to the Bible and our nation. The biblical concept of covenant involves a mutual agreement between God and those who accept the terms of God's invitation to relationship. The terms of this agreement include care for the vulnerable and the creation of a just society, as the prophet Isaiah makes clear: "Cease to do evil; learn to do good. Seek justice; aid the wronged. Defend the orphan; plead for the widow" (Isaiah 1:16–17).

> **The office of president requires the officeholder's unequivocal respect for and commitment to democracy's traditions and their development.**

The notion of covenant also forms the foundation of our nation. Our laws and institutions provide the infrastructure required to fulfill the ideals of a democratic society and protect human and civil rights. This infrastructure is supported by the intangibles of respect, analysis, constructive critique, debate, compromise, and—essential for these—freedom of the press. These are the requisites of a democratic ethos. This is the kind of covenant you have sworn to uphold and protect.

Fareed Zakaria reminds us of what it means to uphold the terms of our democratic covenant: "There is a…tradition in Western politics that, since the Magna Carta in 1215, has centered on the rights of individuals—against arbitrary arrest, religious conversion, censorship of thought. These individual freedoms . . . were eventually protected, not just from the abuse of a tyrant but also from democratic majorities" (*The Washington Post*, December 29, 2016).

The responsibility for democracy now primarily rests in your hands. You cannot renege on its established terms. Anything else would breach the terms of this covenant, betray your office, and blunt the deepest and noblest aspirations of the human spirit.

The office of president requires the officeholder's unequivocal respect for and commitment to democracy's traditions and their development. In your words and your actions, it is paramount that you prove your loyalty to the United States of America and preserve all that it has stood for since its founding several hundred years ago. As an immigrant, a scholar, a Christian, a lesbian, a person of color, and a woman—and for the sake of God's covenant and ours—I expect nothing less of you. We watch!

Dear President Trump, Vice President Pence, Members of the Trump Administration and the 115th Congress,

As an ordained Presbyterian minister and teacher, I love the Bible, as I know many of you do too. Its authority teaches me to respect other authorities, including those who practice science.

The Bible praises Solomon for his knowledge of nature and the way he spoke about trees and animals (1 Kings 4:33). Biblical wisdom draws heavily from the natural realm for its insights, as when Ecclesiastes observes: "A generation goes and a generation comes, but the earth endures forever" (Ecclesiastes 1:4; also Proverbs 30:18–31; Job 38–41; Psalm 104).

The Bible also mandates care for God's creation. When Genesis speaks of humanity having "dominion" over creation (Genesis 1:26–30), it does not mean domination or exploitation of the earth and its creatures. If there were any doubt about that, the very next chapter clarifies that Adam's job is to "serve" and "preserve" the garden (Genesis 2:15). The Bible makes clear that "the earth is the Lord's and all that is in it" (Psalm 24:1). We are only tenants on the vast and beautiful land God has loaned to us (Leviticus 25:23).

> *The only way forward begins with trusting science and acting accordingly.*

Today I worry about our world as ecological crises continue to mount. Make no mistake: these are not hoaxes. As we enter into what some are calling "the long emergency," we are at a crossroads that requires wise and courageous leadership, the kind of leadership that has the long term in view and strives to preserve the health of the planet and "all that is in it." The only way forward begins with trusting science and acting accordingly. Making sure "the earth endures forever" means implementing policies that encourage conservation and a greater reliance on renewable energy. Should not the conservative party of our democracy champion the cause of conservation? Energy independence is a laudable goal, but it can only happen through independence from fossil fuels. An economy without a healthy planet is a failed economy.

I pray that you will exercise the kind of leadership that will ensure the well-being of our planet for future generations. Otherwise, our children and their children will never forgive us.

Dear President Trump, Vice President Pence, Members of the Trump Administration and the 115th Congress,

Humility is the greatest asset of any leader. Those whose roar may seem the loudest at the time, they are the soonest forgotten. Those whose ears are most attuned to the plight of the poor, the marginalized, and the disenfranchised continue to live forever.

Jesus was such a man. Jesus was great not because he garnered the most followers (and he *did* gain the most followers in human history), but because he sat with those who could give him nothing. His power was in both listening and learning, for you become a great teacher by becoming a great learner. Jesus did not sit with the poor simply as a charitable act. From "the least of these" (Matthew 25:40), he learned the core truth of an ancient Hebrew *shalom* system, a system of harmony set forth by God centuries earlier. That system structured love into just laws, not just personal acts of charity.

> *Listening is the first step towards humility and sharing our common humanity.*

When Israelite farmers were commanded to leave forgotten sheaves of wheat or grapes in their fields for the poor (Deuteronomy 24:19), this was an economic regulation designed to provide for those in need. When people were told to leave the edges of their fields unharvested (Leviticus 19:9–10; 23:22), these were labor laws driven by humanitarian and ecological concerns. When citizens were told to provide for the widow, the orphan, and the stranger—the most vulnerable members of the society—this was a command to create a safety net and help those who could not help themselves.

In the biblical period, everyone's spiritual devotion and self-worth were measured by their adherence to these laws and by the extent to which they treated people with justice and compassion. These are the same values that should drive our laws, policy decisions, and daily behavior today.

I urge you to adhere to these same ancient values. I encourage you to sit with people very different from you, especially the poor, and hear their stories. Listening is the first step towards humility and sharing our common humanity. Jesus made himself vulnerable to those from whom he could gain nothing. This is true humility. I challenge you to become a great leader by doing the same.

This image plays with a Hasidic teaching in Letter 41 by Christine Hayes which suggests that people should carry two slips of paper in their pockets: "For my sake the world was created" and "I am but dust and ashes."

RELIGIOUS VOICES: DAY 41–50

LETTER 41 | MARCH 1, 2017

Christine Hayes
Robert F. and Patricia R. Weis Professor of Religious Studies in Classical Judaica, Yale University

LETTER 42 | MARCH 2, 2017

Deirdre Good
Faculty, Stevenson School for Ministry, Episcopal Diocese of Central Pennsylvania

LETTER 43 | MARCH 3, 2017

S. Tamar Kamionkowski
Professor of Biblical Studies, Reconstructionist Rabbinical College

LETTER 44 | MARCH 4, 2017

Judith Plaskow
Professor Emerita of Religious Studies, Manhattan College

LETTER 45 | MARCH 5, 2017

Laura Nasrallah
Professor of New Testament and Early Christianity, Harvard Divinity School

LETTER 46 | MARCH 6, 2017

Amir Hussain
Professor of Theological Studies, Loyola Marymount University

LETTER 47 | MARCH 7, 2017

Susan R. Garrett
Professor of New Testament, Louisville Presbyterian Theological Seminary

LETTER 48 | MARCH 8, 2017

Patrick B. Reyes
Director of Strategic Partnerships for Doctoral Initiatives, Forum for Theological Exploration

LETTER 49 | MARCH 9, 2017

Matthew L. Skinner
Professor of New Testament, Luther Seminary

LETTER 50 | MARCH 10, 2017

Aaron D. Panken
President, Hebrew Union College–Jewish Institute of Religion

Dear President Trump, Vice President Pence, Members of the Trump Administration and the 115th Congress,

The book of Genesis contains two creation myths side by side. Genesis 1 describes the creation of various animal species, reaching a climax with the creation of humankind. Only humans are created—male and female—in God's image, thus signaling their value and dignity and establishing their dominion over the rest of the world.

By contrast, Genesis 2 depicts the creation of a single human from the dust of the earth. This lowly human is responsible for tending and preserving the Garden of Eden, which will be home to the living beings created next.

Religious thinkers have long asserted the importance of heeding the messages inherent in both creation myths. Genesis 1 prioritizes human beings, demanding a fair distribution of resources to ensure their health, welfare, and dignity. But an overemphasis on the majestic human of Genesis 1 can devolve into a devaluation of the rest of creation, providing a warped justification for the unbridled exploitation of nature and the infliction of increasingly irreversible harm on the planet upon which we all depend.

> *Genesis 1 prioritizes humanity . . . but the created world and the life it sustains are also imbued with value.*

The very next chapter, Genesis 2, reminds us that humans possess profound, but not *infinite* value. The created world and the life it sustains are also imbued with value. We humans are but the servants and stewards of an entire universe that existed before us and must continue to sustain life after us.

An old Hasidic tradition instructs people to carry two slips of paper in their pockets: one reflects the majestic human of Genesis 1 and says, "For my sake the world was created"; and the other, in line with the humble servant of Genesis 2, declares, "I am but dust and ashes." The trick is knowing which slip of paper to pull out when.

As you govern, keep these two slips of paper in your pockets. In the face of those who would place profit and power above people, reach for Genesis 1's vision of the supreme value and inalienable dignity of every human—and fight for that truth. In the face of rapacious greed that threatens to destroy the planet, reach for Genesis 2's vision of the humble servant entrusted with the preservation of the created universe—and fight for that truth. Should you reverse them, the consequences will be devastating.

DAY 42, LETTER 42   *Deirdre Good*

Dear President Trump, Vice President Pence, Members of the Trump Administration and the 115th Congress,

Today we look to new leaders to exemplify our democratic values and model how to act in the world. Sacred texts from several ancient cultures esteem the virtues of humility and gentleness as essential and effective modes of leadership.

> *Who better than Jesus proves the benefits of ruling with benevolence and compassion, instead of acting like a tyrannical despot?*

In a Chinese text written over two thousand years ago, the sage of the Tao Te Ching (500–200 BCE) offers some keen advice about leadership: "I have three treasures . . . The first is gentleness, the second is frugality, and the third is not presuming to act like a leader of the world. Gentle, so able to be bold; frugal, so able to be lavish; not presuming to act like a leader of the world, so able to become head of government."

This text contrasts loud and outgoing qualities—being bold, lavish, and self-assertive—with quiet ones—being gentle, frugal, self-effacing. Outgoing qualities by themselves are mere bluster; but when grounded in quiet qualities, they can be deployed far more effectively to benefit the greater good.

In the New Testament, the apostle Paul highlights some of these same values when he praises "love, joy, peace, patience, kindness, generosity, faithfulness, gentleness, and self-control" (Galatians 5:22–23).

The Gospel of Matthew shows how Jesus embodied these quiet virtues. Matthew uses Zechariah 9:9 to describe the arrival of Jesus in Jerusalem as a meek king, "humble and riding on a donkey" (Matthew 21:5). Likewise, Jesus exercises power through gentleness and humility: "Come to me, all you that are weary and are carrying heavy burdens, and I will give you rest . . . for I am gentle and humble in heart, and you will find rest for your souls" (Matthew 11:28–30). Who better than Jesus proves the benefits of ruling with benevolence and compassion, instead of acting like a tyrannical despot?

As you occupy our nation's highest office, which leadership qualities will you demonstrate?

Dear President Trump, Vice President Pence, Members of the Trump Administration and the 115th Congress,

One of the great hallmarks of our democracy is the right to freedom of speech. The very first article of the Bill of Rights states: "Congress shall make no law respecting an establishment of religion, or prohibiting the free exercise thereof; or abridging the freedom of speech, or of the press; or the right of the people peaceably to assemble, and to petition the Government for a redress of grievances."

It is this fundamental American value that ensures the American people, your employers, the right to openly review your performance. This is what supports a robust and diverse press and allows you to tweet without censorship.

Jewish tradition has important wisdom to offer about how we use our speech. Leviticus 19:16 states: "Do not go around as a gossipmonger among your people." The concept of *leshon ha'ra* (evil speech) emerged from this verse. Jewish law forbids all negative speech that may bring emotional, financial, physical, or reputational harm to another person.

> *The gift of speech is one of our most precious and powerful tools.*

There is nothing more powerful than words. In biblical laments, the primary cause of personal anguish was wrongful or hateful speech. Psalm 109:2–3 reads: "For wicked and deceitful mouths are opened against me speaking against me with lying tongues. They beset me with words of hate." The primary cause of suffering in this literature was not physical assault or financial distress, but harmful speech.

Jewish tradition shows that the old adage, "Sticks and stones may break my bones but words will never hurt me," is absolutely false. The gift of speech is one of our most precious and powerful tools. Our speech changes the world. Angry speech generates more anger and fear. Hurtful speech creates pain and divisiveness; but words of kindness and compassion set the stage for unity and security.

As you serve the American people, how will you exercise your right to free speech? What kinds of words will create your legacy?

Dear President Trump, Vice President Pence, Members of the Trump Administration and the 115th Congress,

At this moment in our nation's history when feelings about the issue of immigration are running high and so many immigrants are living in daily fear of deportation, it is useful to reflect on a text that appears in the Hebrew Bible three times, as if to underscore its importance: "You shall not wrong or oppress a stranger, for you were strangers in the land of Egypt" (Exodus 22:20; 23:9; Leviticus 19:33–34).

This command poses a profound moral challenge for the Israelites. It comes at a moment when they are wandering in the desert, not yet settled in their own land with the power to decide how to treat the strangers among them. This biblical law calls on the Israelites to use the *memory* of being outsiders to identify with others in that same position. Rather than reproducing the patterns of domination and subordination that they themselves experienced, the Bible demands the creation of a society in which all are welcome and safe.

This verse lays a moral claim on all of us in the United States today. With the exception of Native Americans, everyone in this country—or everyone's ancestors—came from somewhere else. Even those who came freely, fleeing persecution or looking for greater economic opportunity, had to uproot themselves from their homes, find work, learn a new language and new customs, and generally make their way in a strange land. Many immigrants arrived to find that the reality of the United States did not measure up to their expectations. The streets were not paved with gold. It could be difficult to earn a decent living. They were looked on with suspicion or met with overt discrimination.

> *. . . the Bible demands the creation of a society in which all are welcome and safe.*

What would it mean for each of us—especially those charged with formulating immigration policy—to call to mind our own experiences of migration, or those of our families, and to empathize with a new generation of migrants and refugees trying to reach these shores? How might we use the memories of our families' stories to create the welcome we wish our forebears had encountered? Instead of slamming the door on Syrian refugees and people from certain Muslim-majority nations, how can we use our own histories to forge a new relationship with the strangers among us?

Laura Nasrallah

Dear President Trump, Vice President Pence, Members of the Trump Administration and the 115th Congress,

"Aliens and sojourners" (1 Peter 2:11, Hebrews 11:13). In the New Testament, early Christians sometimes used this phrase, feeling themselves to be immigrants as they sought new ways to form themselves into a people. Throughout American history, various Christian groups also adopted the language of "aliens and sojourners" to think about their identity.

"A city on a hill" (Matthew 5:14). Attributed to Jesus, this phrase was also used by John Winthrop in 1630 to describe the pioneering work of the Puritans who made their way to Massachusetts. They knew, as Winthrop said, that "the eyes of all people are upon us" and would judge the success or failure of this radical idea of a community based on how that community valued justice, mercy, and humility.

Now, a heavy-handed, self-satisfied claim to be a city on a hill can be problematic; and no single religion's ideas can define our nation, since we hold to the separation of church and state. Yet this idea of being aliens and sojourners and this longing to be a city upon a hill— these are important parts of our country's history and important models for us now. These quotations from Christian scripture, and the varied religions within the United States, when at their best, give us a glimpse of utopian thought. They give us glimpses of governance done right, of justice enacted, of diverse peoples gathered together in celebration.

> *. . . the varied religions within the United States, when at their best, give us glimpses of . . . governance done right, of justice enacted, of diverse peoples gathered together in celebration.*

I speak not only as a biblical scholar and historian, but as a member of a family in which two were born in this country and two were born elsewhere. In the U.S., we found a safe haven and an escape from violence fed by politics and religion. Many of you have similar stories from your own families, whether recent or in generations past.

As you govern in this new administration, I ask that you shift your policies to value the alien and sojourner who wish to enter into the vision of America. I ask that you respect and celebrate the variety of religious voices that enthusiastically and critically support our nation, offering new visions of how we can be a city on a hill. As Winthrop said, "the eyes of all people are upon us."

Amir Hussain

Dear President Trump, Vice President Pence, Members of the Trump Administration and the 115th Congress,

Peace be upon you, and the mercy and blessings of God. I write to you as an American Muslim who has spent his personal and professional life engaged in interfaith dialogue and comparative theology. You probably know that the commandment repeated more than any other in the Torah is the charge not to mistreat the stranger: "You shall not oppress a stranger. You know the feelings of the stranger, for you were strangers in the land of Egypt" (Exodus 23:9).

> *The Qur'an is explicit that our doing good and showing beauty is not limited to our family, but also applies to those in need . . .*

You also know from the Gospels, especially from Matthew 25:31–46 (the parable of the great banquet), that Jesus commands us to care for the stranger: "For I was hungry and you gave me food, I was thirsty and you gave me drink, I was a stranger and you welcomed me, I was naked and you clothed me, I was sick and you took care of me, I was in prison and you visited me." In the original Greek text of the New Testament, the "you" is always in the plural. Jesus commands all of us, together, to care for the stranger.

What you may not know is that the same biblical teachings are found in the Qur'an: "Serve God and do not associate anything with God, and be good to both your parents, and to the near of kin, and the orphans, and the needy, and the neighbor who is near and the neighbor who is farther away, and the companion by your side, and the traveler, and those whom your right hands possess; surely God does not love the one who is proud, boastful" (Qur'an 4:36). What I have translated as "and be good" is even more powerful in the Arabic original, which reads as "do something beautiful" for the people it then lists. The Qur'an is explicit that our doing good and showing beauty is not limited to our family, but also applies to those in need, whether they are literally our neighbor or someone far away from us.

I ask you, with all respect and humility, to follow these commandments in our sacred texts. In doing so, we live out the best of our ideals, both as religious persons and as Americans. We will be judged, as Jesus warned us, by how we treat the least of our brothers and sisters.

Dear President Trump, Vice President Pence, Members of the Trump Administration and the 115th Congress,

New Testament authors disagreed about how Christians should relate to governing authorities. Their ancient disagreements about "the powers that be" remain surprisingly relevant today.

> " *. . . ancient disagreements about "the powers that be" remain surprisingly relevant today.*

The apostle Paul wrote: "Let everyone be subordinate to the governing authorities; for there is no authority except from God, and those authorities that exist have been instituted by God" (Romans 13:1). Some Christians who resent current expressions of opposition to our government quote this verse to oppose the Black Lives Matter movement, women's marches across the country, or protests against the president's travel ban.

In contrast, Luke recounted an act of civil disobedience by Peter and the apostles, who defied the authorities trying to silence them: "We must obey God rather than any human authority" (Acts 5:29). In the book of Revelation, the prophet John compared oppressive authorities in his own day to a beast who wars against God's people while inducing blind obedience from others: "They worshipped the beast, saying, 'Who is like the beast, and who can fight against it?'" (Revelation 13:4). John exhorted Christians to resist the authoritarian beast by refusing to cooperate with its orders.

Despite their differences, all three New Testament authors shared certain underlying assumptions. They all believed that the powers and principalities have a spiritual dimension that is much bigger than any individual who occupies a particular office. They all recognized that these powers sometimes serve good purposes, and sometimes evil ones. They all insisted that although Christians may respect earthly forms of power, God alone deserves their worship and ultimate submission.

In the time of the Bible and today, governing authorities are tasked with helping people flourish by maintaining just laws. When they do, they should be supported. But sometimes the desire for self-preservation or self-aggrandizement displaces the intent to serve the noble goals of a given institution. When leaders no longer act as good stewards of the authority entrusted to them, they should be challenged.

For Christians, Scripture teaches that the United States and its leaders ought never claim our ultimate allegiance. God comes first. The task of Christian citizens—indeed all people of faith—is to call governing authorities to fulfill God's purpose of bringing about justice, mercy, and peace.

Dear President Trump, Vice President Pence, Members of the Trump Administration and the 115th Congress,

Reflecting on "the greatest generation"—the leaders who lived through the Great Depression, fought in World War II, and breathed life back into American society in the civil rights era—Tom Brokaw writes that "they stayed true to their values of personal responsibility, duty, honor, and faith" (*The Greatest Generation*). As you serve our nation, what will you do to support the next greatest generation? How do you intend to uphold these values of personal responsibility, duty, honor, and faith?

> *Religious leaders of the greatest generation . . . counseled the afflicted and powerful alike to advocate, support, and love the marginalized.*

With the signing of executive orders that bar people like my family from immigrating to the U.S., communities feel persecuted. With an "America first" agenda and inflammatory rhetoric that has led to racial tensions, xenophobia, and violence, communities feel threatened. With the proposal of fewer health and human services to serve the poor and vulnerable, communities feel betrayed.

Religious leaders of the greatest generation—Martin Luther King Jr., Cesar Chavez, Abraham Joshua Heschel, Fred Shuttlesworth, Fannie Lou Hamer, Thomas Merton, Howard Thurman, Dorothy Day, and others—counseled the afflicted and powerful alike to advocate, support, and love the marginalized. They sought to actualize the pervasive scriptural mandate to protect and love the stranger (Leviticus 19:33–34) and to "let justice roll down like water" (Amos 5:24). They worked tirelessly to better local and national communities and to help the nation discern and calibrate its moral fiber.

Should you want to embrace the values of the greatest generation, I leave you with the following counsel: ¡Basta! Enough of the violent and hateful rhetoric against minorities, especially Latinx communities on both sides of the border. ¡Basta! Stop targeting religious groups and take responsibility for how your policies and public persona have emboldened hate groups across this country. ¡Basta! Enough publicly antagonizing world leaders with our military power. Every war is a war on future generations. ¡Basta! Stop signing executive orders and pushing policies that limit access to education, health care, and human services for racial, ethnic, and religious minorities.

My generation has the responsibility of creating the conditions in which future generations can thrive. They are the next greatest generation. I urge you to join us in this work.

Matthew L. Skinner

Dear President Trump, Vice President Pence, Members of the Trump Administration and the 115th Congress,

The biblical faith I profess and teach reminds me that sometimes outsiders can perceive truth and virtue in ways that insiders could not dream of seeing.

> "
>
> *We need people from outside our borders and dominant culture to help us see new manifestations of familiar American values.*

To the ancient Hebrews, Rahab was a foreigner with little to offer besides a safe haven for spies. But she proved to have clearer vision than the spies, whose faith she reinvigorated (Joshua 2). Although the prophet Amos lived in the southern kingdom of Judah, when called by God, he ventured to the neighboring kingdom of Israel to speak uncomfortable truths, even to the king and his shortsighted advisors (Amos 7:10–17).

A Syrophoenician woman, someone with almost nothing in common with Jesus except their shared humanity, refused to let him say no when she begged him to deliver her daughter from horrible suffering (Mark 7:24–30). An Ethiopian man, passing through Judea, inferred that he, too, could be baptized just like any other member of the young Christian church (Acts 8:26–40). A slave named Rhoda, although her Christian owners and their friends mocked her knowledge, nevertheless persisted and rightly maintained that what she had seen was true (Acts 12:12–17).

The U.S. has a complicated history when it comes to how the dominant culture regards "outsiders." Too often we have treated outsiders as people to exclude, resist, shame, exploit, dominate, and enslave. My faith requires me to denounce ideologies and policies that perpetuate these ugly legacies of the American experiment—those promulgated in the past and those proposed today.

That being said, I do not expect you and your programs to show respect and hospitality to outsiders just for *biblical* reasons. I urge you to embrace a similar *political* wisdom because it benefits America. America flourishes whenever it promotes and refines its commitments to freedom and opportunity for all people. Supposed outsiders actually can perceive, extend, revamp, and even correct the nation's ideals in insightful and innovative ways. When our politics deny this truth, we put ourselves at risk of stifling and corrupting our loftiest values.

Insularity promotes error and hastens death. We need people from outside our borders and dominant culture to help us see new manifestations of familiar values. "We the people" is an ever expanding and changing group. As our notion of "we" grows, our values shine all the more brightly.

Dear President Trump, Vice President Pence, Members of the Trump Administration and the 115th Congress,

The advent of each new administration calls for the broad re-creation of our country every four to eight years. Such moments of re-creation offer an opportunity to learn from the biblical creation story itself.

Genesis 1 narrates the well-known creation myth that culminates on the sixth day with the fashioning of the first human being. An early Jewish interpretation highlights two essential aspects of this tale: "A single human being was created to teach you that anyone who destroys a single life, it is as if they have destroyed an entire world; and anyone who sustains a single life, it is as if they have sustained an entire world." Also, only a single human was created to teach that "no one may claim ancestry that is greater than anyone else's" (Mishnah Sanhedrin 4:5).

> *. . . inherent in your leadership is the sacred possibility of sustaining the entire world . . .by constructively imagining how each constituent's life might be improved . . .*

This gets to the core of what it means to govern a nation in which all citizens are created equal. In the decisions you make, you must take into account each and every human being affected by your words and actions. This ancient text reminds us of the manifold ways that people in power and the policies they create can destroy the lives of others: by denying them health care, tearing apart their families through wanton deportation and travel bans, polluting their environment, negating their humanity, or downgrading their education. Each of these acts is tantamount to the destruction of the whole world.

But also inherent in your leadership is the sacred possibility of sustaining the entire world: by rising above prejudice, polarization, and hatred, by working for unity and coherence, and by constructively imagining how each constituent's life might be improved through collaborative, respectful, intentional endeavors.

The mishnah concludes by reminding us that no one's ancestry—and thus no one's humanity—is greater than anyone else's. No American deserves to suffer the disgrace of discrimination, whether due to gender, race, religion, sexuality, economic status, or any other facet of their individuality.

Our government has always been a global beacon of pluralism and respect for others. I pray that will continue in your administration. We are counting on you.

On February 16, 2017, just twenty-eight days into the campaign, our online subscriber tally reached 2,017. The number was significant not only because it marked a spike in readership, but because it represented the year of the campaign.

RELIGIOUS VOICES: DAY 51–60

LETTER 51 | MARCH 11, 2017

Jennifer T. Kaalund
Assistant Professor of Religious Studies,
Iona College

LETTER 52 | MARCH 12, 2017

Aaron Koller
Associate Professor of Near Eastern
and Jewish Studies, Yeshiva University

LETTER 53 | MARCH 13, 2017

Greg Carey
Professor of New Testament, Lancaster
Theological Seminary

LETTER 54 | MARCH 14, 2017

Mai-Anh Le Tran
Associate Professor of Religious
Education and Practical Theology,
Garrett-Evangelical Theological Seminary

LETTER 55 | MARCH 15, 2017

Jennifer Wright Knust
Associate Professor of New Testament
and Christian Origins, Boston University

LETTER 56 | MARCH 16, 2017

Miguel H. Díaz
The John Courtney Murray University
Chair in Public Service, Loyola University
Chicago, Retired U.S. Ambassador to
the Holy See

LETTER 57 | MARCH 17, 2017

Teresa Delgado
Professor and Chair of Religious Studies
& Peace and Justice Studies Director,
Iona College

LETTER 58 | MARCH 18, 2017

Raj Nadella
Assistant Professor of New Testament,
Columbia Theological Seminary

LETTER 59 | MARCH 19, 2017

Stephen Breck Reid
Professor of Christian Scriptures,
George W. Truett Theological Seminary
of Baylor University

LETTER 60 | MARCH 20, 2017

Jeffrey H. Tigay
Emeritus Ellis Professor of Hebrew and
Semitic Languages and Literatures,
University of Pennsylvania

Dear President Trump, Vice President Pence, Members of the Trump Administration and the 115th Congress,

Beginnings are a time of reflection. In the New Testament, the Gospels provide reflections of a people troubled by their uncertain future. They look back on earlier events and project a hopeful future informed by values and principles of the past.

The Gospel of Luke presents such a beginning in Jesus' inaugural sermon. Jesus most clearly articulates his mission statement when, reciting Isaiah 61:1–2 in the synagogue, he declares: "The Spirit of the Lord is upon me, because he has anointed me to bring good news to the poor. He sent me to proclaim release to the captives and recovery of sight to the blind, to let the oppressed go free, to proclaim the year of the Lord's favor" (Luke 4:18–19). Thus, Jesus' first public declaration expresses concern for justice, specifically for the poor and the oppressed.

> *Luke reminds us that the Lord's favor is preserved for those who are devoted to justice . . .*

In antiquity and today, the poor are not simply those disadvantaged economically, but also those who lack honor, prestige, and power. Jesus came, was anointed, and eventually died for such individuals. And yet, the Gospel of Luke does not simply offer a narrative that champions the underdog, it also provides a cautionary tale to the rich and the proud. Luke reminds us that the Lord's favor is preserved for those who are devoted to justice and who respond to the call to work on the behalf of marginalized and vulnerable people. This message is rooted in the Hebrew Bible's principles of love, mercy, and righteousness.

As we boldly proclaim who we are as a country, let us reflect on our past. The poem inscribed on the Statue of Liberty, an emblem of freedom and hospitality, reads: "Give me your tired, your poor, your huddled masses, yearning to breathe free." This iconic American monument reminds us that this country welcomes the outcast and downtrodden.

As you begin the task of leading our country, take to heart the principles advocated by Jesus and later embraced by our nation. Make sure these ancient values guide your purpose and inform our continued struggle to see justice and liberty for all realized in our country and our world.

Aaron Koller

Dear President Trump, Vice President Pence, Members of the Trump Administration and the 115th Congress,

The great religions of the world have accumulated thousands of years of wisdom on the subject of leadership. Jewish texts speak often about power and its uses, and these texts continue to speak with a clear voice in the modern world.

> *True wisdom, power, and honor, the Mishnah teaches, come from humility, openness, and self-control.*

A mishnah in Avot, a rabbinic text from nearly two thousand years ago, reflects on qualities that humans, especially elected officials, aspire to obtain: wisdom, power, and honor. The rabbis offer a paradoxical definition of these qualities: "Who is wise? One who learns from every person. Who is powerful? One who controls his impulses. Who is honored? One who honors all people" (Avot 4:1). True wisdom, power, and honor, the Mishnah teaches, come from humility, openness, and self-control.

These lessons are echoed in modern studies of leadership. Contemporary research shows that leaders who know how to listen, respect others, and act with restraint can better bring people together and accomplish their goals. Daniel Goleman's classic article on leadership in the *Harvard Business Review*, for example, identifies empathy, social skills, and self-restraint as critical qualities for successful leaders.

The country is still hurting from a long and bruising campaign and a divisive start to a new administration. This has exposed deep divisions among our people. We need leaders who demonstrate these qualities:

- a willingness to listen to and learn from all people,
- the capacity to demonstrate power through restraint,
- and an ability to command honor and respect by doling out honor and respect to all those who deserve it.

We all yearn for leaders who exemplify these traits and can unify the country, bringing wisdom to a complex and challenging world. We hope and pray that your administration can succeed in bringing needed leadership in a complicated time. The teachings of our ancient texts can illuminate the way.

Dear President Trump, Vice President Pence, Members of the Trump Administration and the 115th Congress,

Having won an election in an extremely contentious campaign, you now serve as leaders and representatives for all Americans. I can only imagine the sense of honor and accountability that comes with that reality. This leads me to think about how my own religious tradition, Christianity, might speak to what it means to govern in such a divided culture.

In the Sermon on the Mount, speaking from a deep reservoir of Jewish wisdom, Jesus voices God's blessing to all sorts of people: "Blessed are the poor . . . Blessed are the meek . . . Blessed are those who hunger and thirst for righteousness" (Matthew 5:3–6). This attention to those who are crushed by despair, grief, and the absence of justice suggests that a key measure of a leader is what he or she does for the poor and the powerless.

Jesus goes on to offer his interpretation of the law of Moses, starting with the prohibition of murder in the Ten Commandments. Jesus declares: "You have heard that it was said to those of ancient times, 'You shall not murder'; and 'whoever murders shall be liable to judgment.' But I say to you that if you are angry with a brother or sister, you will be liable to judgment; and if you insult a brother or sister, you will be liable to the council; and if you say, 'You fool,' you will be liable to the hell of fire" (Matthew 5:21–22).

> **" Jesus teaches that we stand under God's judgment . . . if we insult or belittle another human being.**

Jesus teaches that we stand under God's judgment not just if we kill a human life, but if we insult or belittle another human being. When we demean our brother or sister, we offend the God who created them. Since every person carries the image of God (Genesis 1:26–27), to harm a human being physically or emotionally is to mar the divine presence.

Too often our political culture is defined by insults and half-truths. By demonstrating respect for our opponents and detractors, we model a new way of living together in this society, one that favors compassion over violence and honor over humiliation. My prayer is that our elected leaders will foster a robust public conversation in a way that honors all people created in God's image.

Dear President Trump, Vice President Pence, Members of the Trump Administration and the 115th Congress,

"Not many of you should become teachers . . . for you know that we who teach will be judged with greater strictness" (James 3:1). This ethical exhortation from an early Christian teacher speaks to those of us who occupy positions of public leadership today. Teachers and leaders in public life—what some educators call "leading learners"—are cautioned that we will be judged with greater strictness.

This is not a double standard, but rather a more profound one. The true test of our fitness for public service—what many Christians know as "servant leadership"—rests not on pedigree or personal triumph, but on the integrity of our character, the openness of our vision, and the consequences that our actions will bear upon all lives under our care, especially the most vulnerable ones. For this reason, both religions and nation-states yearn for leaders who pursue Goodness, who lead and learn with moral force rather than brute might.

> *. . . religions and nation-states yearn for leaders who pursue Goodness, who lead and learn with moral force rather than brute might.*

Christians glean from their Judaic heritage many powerful elements of such moral force: justice, mercy, and humility (Micah 6:8), to be practiced with faith, hope, and love (1 Corinthians 13:13). The call to live and lead with such moral force is ever potent in this liturgical season of Lent, when we are invited into a spiritual journey with a teacher, a first-century Galilean Jew, who protested repressive political and religious rule. He taught followers to deprivatize their notions of daily bread and to cultivate an alternative imagination for communal well-being. Then and now, the followers of Jesus remember him as one who was persecuted and executed for insisting upon a ministry of freedom that unbinds people from the powers and principalities that relish in deals of death and condemnation. This is the very freedom encapsulated in 2 Corinthians 3:17, which the president once cited.

Indeed, not many of us should lead, but let those who seek such awesome responsibility do so in pursuit of Goodness. Let us heed the words of Confucius, another wise teacher, who cautioned leaders in *The Analects*: "Govern the people by regulations, keep order among them by chastisements, and they will flee from you, and lose all self-respect. Govern them by moral force . . . and they will keep their self-respect and come to you of their own accord."

Dear President Trump, Vice President Pence, Members of the Trump Administration and the 115th Congress,

When my Great-Grandma Thorson (née Rasmussen) was in her eighties, we took her to Washington, D.C. An immigrant from Denmark, she began her American life as a cook for Minnesotan farmhands, where she met my Great-Grandfather Thorson, and together they moved to Iowa to start a farm. The farm was auctioned off during the Depression, so the young family headed west to California, nearly starving on the way. "Rich people lied," Great-Grandpa Thorson told my mom, "and the rest of us went hungry."

> " *. . . the proposition that all are created equal . . . is neither easily embraced nor easily defended.*

Thanks to the New Deal, perseverance, and a whole lot of luck, the Thorson family rebuilt their lives. When Great-Grandma visited the Lincoln Memorial, she wept, grateful for a country that, in the end, had sustained her and her family.

Visiting the Memorial again recently, I gazed at President Lincoln, heavy in his chair, and thought of Great-Grandma in her wheelchair. I was reminded that the proposition that all are created equal—an idea enshrined in the Bible and the Declaration of Independence—is neither easily embraced nor easily defended. I was reminded that "government of the people, by the people, for the people" can, in fact, perish from the earth.

As elected leaders, as you fulfill your pledge to preserve, protect, and defend the U.S. Constitution, I urge you to claim the best of our shared American heritage, just as I pledge to do the same: In honor of my Baptist forebears, I will do my part to protect religious liberty. No religious community, the Revolutionary Era Baptists argued, should be targeted for discrimination. In honor of my immigrant ancestry, I will welcome the stranger and show hospitality to everyone seeking a better life in this country. In honor of my Great-Uncle Hans Rasmussen, whose WPA-constructed bridge still stands in Story City, Iowa, I intend to build bridges, not walls. In honor of Great-Grandpa Thorson, I promise to "speak truth from [my] heart" (Psalm 15:2), even at my own disadvantage. In honor of Great-Grandma Thorson, whose well-worn Danish Bible rests on my desk, I will endeavor to live out a faith that pursues healing for the sick, food for the hungry, and justice for all (Matthew 13; Luke 4).

I hold you, my elected leaders, accountable for what you have promised. May we all be held accountable for the promises we make and the heritages we claim.

DAY 56, LETTER 56 *Miguel H. Díaz*

Dear President Trump, Vice President Pence, Members of the Trump Administration and the 115th Congress,

I had the privilege and honor of serving our country as U.S. ambassador to the Holy See in Rome from 2009 to 2012. I write to you as a concerned fellow American and as a Cuban exile who at the age of eight, together with my parents, left everything behind to join the multitude of immigrants that Lady Liberty has welcomed from across the Straits of Florida.

> *Whether concrete or ideological, walls pose a great threat to democracy.*

A few years ago, while serving as ambassador, I was asked at an international conference in Spain why some Americans favored building a wall with our southern neighbor after our nation had led the efforts to tear down the Berlin Wall. The Berlin Wall, which separated a single people, now stands as a symbol of unnecessary and unnatural separation among persons and communities. Whether concrete or ideological, walls pose a great threat to democracy. They undermine America's ability to stand for God-given human differences and the fundamental human right to life of all peoples.

In his 2015 historic speech to Congress, Pope Francis cautioned: "A political society endures when it seeks, as a vocation, to satisfy common needs by stimulating the growth of all its members, especially those in situations of greater vulnerability or risk." The pope has condemned what he has characterized as "the globalization of human indifference."

As Americans, we have fought hard at home and abroad to defend vulnerable populations, denouncing indifference constructed on the basis of race, gender, sexual orientation, physical ability, religious affiliation, political ideologies, and immigration status. This work must continue.

I pray for you, Mr. President, and for all our leaders, that you will listen and respond to the cries of the "huddled masses . . . the wretched refuse . . . the homeless, tempest-tost," especially the undocumented immigrants in our land. We, the people, need you to set aside politics, lift your lamp beside the golden door, and speak the truth. Remember, as the Gospel tells us, "the truth will set us free" (John 8:32).

The world is watching and eagerly waits to see if compassionate and just leadership will emerge from the capital of "the land of the free and the home of the brave."

DAY 57, LETTER 57   *Teresa Delgado*

Dear President Trump, Vice President Pence, Members of the Trump Administration and the 115th Congress,

As a young Puerto Rican girl growing up in the Roman Catholic Church and attending Roman Catholic school from kindergarten through twelfth grade, I often heard a popular song at Mass that repeated the following refrain: "Let there be peace on earth, and let it begin with me." I always loved this song, with its inspiring yet haunting melody. It usually made me cry in silent repentance, reminding me in my combative and impulsive youth that peace rarely began with me.

In my life's journey—through college and graduate school, as a wife, mother, theologian, and teacher—I have sought the wisdom of those who seem to embody this message of Matthew's Gospel: "Blessed are the peacemakers, for they shall be called the children of God" (Matthew 5:9). In his blog, "What Is Written in Our Hearts," David Cloutier affirms Pope Francis' call for us to reflect on this section of the Beatitudes, for these words "say to us, find the merciful, find the poor in spirit, find the peacemakers, find those who suffer for their faith . . . and imitate them."

> " . . . surround yourself with those worthy of imitation in the work of justice and peace.

We are blessed with peacemakers, to imitate in our time: Mohandas Gandhi, Dorothy Day, Cesar Chavez, Martin Luther King Jr., Thich Nhat Hanh, Anna Mae Aquash, Abraham Joshua Heschel, Tawakkul Karman. Walking different spiritual paths, these leaders sought peace with every step on a journey illumined by a striving toward justice. As Pope Paul VI said, "If you want peace, work for justice."

Like them, we have a choice, as the song goes, to "take each moment, and live each moment, in peace eternally." That means surrounding ourselves—in body and spirit—with peacemakers worthy of our imitation, reminding us of our unique capacity to do the work of justice and peace in our world without exception. If we are to be called God's children, nothing less is expected of us.

I pray that in your unique capacity as leaders of our country—but more importantly as children of God—you will surround yourselves with those worthy of imitation in the work of justice and peace. That way, we can proclaim together, "Let there be peace on earth. And let it begin with me."

Dear President Trump, Vice President Pence, Members of the Trump Administration and the 115th Congress,

In Luke 14:15–24, Jesus narrates the parable of someone who planned a great banquet that did not include the disadvantaged. The invited guests—the privileged—made various excuses to not attend. We can never know if their excuses were genuine and why they did not attend; but we do know the implications of their actions. Faced with the embarrassment of an empty banquet hall, the host invited those originally excluded: "the poor, the crippled, the blind, the lame." Luke's parable reiterates the moral imperative of taking a stand in support of the underprivileged. In today's context, it challenges the powerful to leverage their privilege in order to advocate for those excluded from economic and social structures.

> *Paradoxically, by siding with the powerless, one gains and maintains power.*

The United States has always taken pride in its legacy of employing power and clout on the global platform to advocate for oppressed groups such as religious or ethnic minorities and refugees. Our troubled history notwithstanding, America has committed resources and armed forces in order to protect human rights in other parts of the world. This cherished history reflects America's commitment to defending life and liberty for the marginalized, regardless of their identity.

So how can a country that prides itself on championing religious freedom and human rights welcome some refugees but prohibit others based on religion? How can we justify turning our backs on the vulnerable when they knock on our doors fleeing violence and persecution?

This quintessential American value of welcoming the "huddled masses yearning to breathe free" is not just a moral principle built on idealism. Paradoxically, by siding with the powerless, one gains and maintains power. Paul teaches this when he shows how Jesus sacrificed his divine privilege in order to identify with the least among us and, consequently, was exalted to the highest place (Philippians 2:5–11).

This ethos of solidarity has made America a global leader and granted us immense power and influence. I urge you to follow this biblical wisdom and practice compassion. A nation's character is judged by the extent of its commitment to "the lowly and the destitute" (Psalm 82:3). Our future and our fortunes depend on it.

Dear President Trump, Vice President Pence, Members of the Trump Administration and the 115th Congress,

As you embark on a great adventure of service to the American people, I encourage you to recall President Ronald Reagan's use of the Russian proverb: "Trust but verify." Remember that before Reagan and the Russian proverb, the Hebrew prophet Micah and Jesus taught some simple metrics for verifying that our religious and civic language matches the policies we enact.

Micah describes a vision of an age marked by widespread peace and tranquility. Instead of spending precious resources on weapons, Micah declares that nations "shall beat their swords into plowshares" and "not learn war any more." Security will bring about shared prosperity: "Everyone shall sit under their own vine and under their own fig tree, and none shall make them afraid" (Micah 4:3–4).

> *. . . the story of Lazarus provides a cautionary tale that refutes the saying, "A rising tide raises all ships."*

Micah challenges "trickle-down" economics. Likewise, the story of Lazarus provides a cautionary tale that refutes the saying, "A rising tide raises all ships." In Luke 16:19–31, an elegantly dressed rich man feasts sumptuously each day while neglecting Lazarus, a poor man at his gate. Lazarus is reduced to trying to survive on the scraps that fall from the rich man's table.

How many more people like Lazarus will we see at our gates once budget cuts to HUD lead to an increase in homelessness? With an end to funding for programs like Meals on Wheels, how many more folks like Lazarus will be forced to beg for food or go hungry? When millions lose their health insurance, how many people will we see like Lazarus, who was covered with sores and died from his illness?

While Lazarus receives no help from the rich man, he merits divine favor. When he dies, he is "carried away by the angels to be with Abraham." The rich man, on the other hand, dies and goes to Hades. Once he realizes the folly of his ways, it is too late. When he petitions to warn his relatives and friends, Abraham replies: "If they do not hear Moses and the prophets, neither will they be convinced if someone should rise from the dead" (Luke 16:31).

The "America First" budget does not match our religious or civic values. We can and must do better.

Dear President Trump, Vice President Pence, Members of the Trump Administration and the 115th Congress,

There is a perennial debate about the proper method for interpreting the Constitution, particularly whether it should be interpreted strictly—only as perceived to be intended by its authors—or loosely—with its interpretation evolving as the times and circumstances change.

> **" The Constitution must be a flexible, living instrument so that we as a nation can thrive.**

In Jewish tradition, the Torah occupies the same position as the Constitution in America. It is instructive that throughout history, Jewish legal scholars frequently chose a loose construction approach, despite the fact that they regarded the Torah as the word of God.

A classic example appears in the interpretation of the famous law that prescribes "an eye for an eye" as punishment for wounding another person. The law was originally meant literally, as Leviticus 24:19–20 makes clear: "If anyone maims his fellow, as he has done so shall it be done to him: fracture for fracture, eye for eye, tooth for tooth. The injury he inflicted on another shall be inflicted on him."

Yet in the Talmud, the classic work of Jewish jurisprudence, the Bible's original meaning is replaced by an interpretation that insists the law does *not* require the perpetrator to suffer the same injury, but rather to make *monetary* compensation for any injuries (Mishnah Bava Kamma 8:1). The perception of what constitutes cruel and unusual punishment evolved by the period of the Talmud. Because the talmudic rabbis could not believe that a benevolent God intended a punishment as harsh as the literal meaning of the Bible implied, they reinterpreted the law.

The Talmud maintains that even when the intentions of the law's author—God—are absolutely certain, God cannot dictate how humans apply the law in specific cases (Babylonian Talmud Bava Metsia 59b). The meaning of a law in any particular case cannot be limited to what its *author* would have said. Instead, its application must comport with what the human judges decide the law means in light of the circumstances of their own time.

American society would benefit from a similar approach to our Constitution, one that insists that the interpretation of laws must be consistent with contemporary values and the overall welfare of contemporary society. A law whose literal meaning does more harm than good must be reinterpreted. The Constitution must be a flexible, living instrument so that we as a nation can thrive.

Letter 9 inspired Vicki Gray-Wolfe's illustration "Refugee Boy."
Ellen Armour writes: "May we . . . commit ourselves to greeting refugees
with love and faith, rather than rejecting them with hate and fear."

RELIGIOUS VOICES: DAY 61–70

LETTER 61 | MARCH 21, 2017

Jennifer L. Koosed
Professor of Religious Studies,
Albright College

LETTER 62 | MARCH 22, 2017

Naomi Koltun-Fromm
Associate Professor of Religion,
Haverford College

LETTER 63 | MARCH 23, 2017

Phyllis Trible
Baldwin Professor Emerita of Sacred
Literature, Union Theological Seminary

LETTER 64 | MARCH 24, 2017

J. B. Haws
Associate Professor of Church History,
Brigham Young University

LETTER 65 | MARCH 25, 2017

Tammi J. Schneider
Professor of Religion, Claremont
Graduate University

LETTER 66 | MARCH 26, 2017

Shawnee M. Daniels-Sykes
Associate Professor of Theology
and Ethics, Mount Mary University

LETTER 67 | MARCH 27, 2017

Neomi DeAnda
Associate Professor of Religious Studies,
University of Dayton

LETTER 68 | MARCH 28, 2017

Gregory E. Sterling
The Reverend Henry L. Slack Dean
& Lillian Claus Professor of New
Testament, Yale Divinity School

LETTER 69 | MARCH 29, 2017

Brian Rainey
Assistant Professor of Old Testament,
Princeton Theological Seminary

LETTER 70 | MARCH 30, 2017

Jeremy V. Cruz
Assistant Professor of Theology and
Religious Studies, St. John's University

DAY 61, LETTER 61

Jennifer L. Koosed

Dear President Trump, Vice President Pence, Members of the Trump Administration and the 115th Congress,

Creating a family is a great responsibility, with deeply personal choices about when and how we bring new life into the world. In 1965, 1972, and 1973, the Supreme Court established a constitutional right to privacy and forbade the state from intruding in family planning. Many people of faith agree with these decisions and insist that matters of birth control and abortion should be left to a woman, in conversation with her family, doctor, or clergy if desired.

> *Our advocacy and efforts should be focused on creating a world where women are safe and have access to the services and support needed to nurture life . . .*

While a few poetic texts in the Bible pay tribute to God's connection to individuals in a "mother's womb" (such as Psalms 22:11; 139:13), only one biblical law concerns fetal life. Exodus 21:22–25 describes the consequences when two men fight and accidentally injure a pregnant woman. If the woman miscarries, a fine is levied. If further harm comes to the woman, equal harm must be meted out: If she dies, the death penalty—"life for life"—must be paid. This text makes a clear distinction between *fetal* life and *human* life: If a fetus is killed, damage has been done, but murder has not been committed. From this passage, Judaism derives its position: not only are there times when abortions *can* be performed (generally rape, incest, statutory rape, great emotional distress), but sometimes they *must* be carried out (when the woman's physical or mental health is threatened) (Mishnah Oholot 7:6; Talmud Sanhedrin 72b).

I am not suggesting that U.S. law should mirror biblical or rabbinic law. In fact, I am suggesting the opposite: that no law concerning birth control or abortion should reflect any particular religion's ethic. It remains fundamental not only to our right to privacy, but also to freedom of religion, for abortion and birth control to remain accessible and legal so that all Americans are free to follow the wisdom of their religious tradition and the guidance of their conscience.

Our advocacy and efforts should be focused on creating a world where women are safe and have access to the services and support needed to nurture life in the way that each woman "awesomely and wonderfully made" (Psalm 139:14) decides is best.

Dear President Trump, Vice President Pence, Members of the Trump Administration and the 115th Congress,

Through the Establishment Clause of the Bill of Rights, our Founding Fathers enshrined the principle of the shared humanity of all citizens, no matter their creed. This document mandates that our most closely held religious truths cannot be used to control the lives of other citizens through government legislation: "Congress shall make no law respecting an establishment of religion, or prohibiting the free exercise thereof."

> **For the sake of the greater good, we need to strive to understand one another and respect our differences . . .**

In America, we rule not without religion, but with a recognition that people worship in different ways and, more broadly, live in this world in different ways. This innovative American value allows all citizens, no matter how or what they believe, to flourish and contribute to this great country.

Our Founding Fathers were wise enough to recognize that strongly held religious beliefs can stand in the way of good governance. This is especially true when legislation involves religious or ideological notions not shared by all Americans, as is the case with contentious issues like abortion. Democracy and the respect for religious differences upon which it was founded necessitate compromise.

The ancient rabbis Hillel and Shammai model respect for diversity of opinion. These first-century sages and their followers disagreed on many of the fundamentals of Jewish law and practice; yet they did not disparage each other's different rulings. The pages of the Mishnah and Talmud preserve their opposing opinions side by side. In one particular case, they disagreed on who should be allowed to marry whom (Mishnah Yebamot 1.4; Babylonian Talmud Yebamot 14a). Nevertheless, those ideological disputes did not prevent their followers from living together and engaging each other in meaningful dialogue on this and other issues. Why? Because survival and communal unity demanded that they learn to disagree amicably and to live with mutual respect.

We in America would do well to learn from both our Founding Fathers and the ancient rabbis. For the sake of the greater good, we need to strive to understand one another and respect our differences, even when we "agree to disagree."

Dear President Trump, Vice President Pence, Members of the Trump Administration and the 115th Congress,

Shock. Disgust. Depression. Devastation.

A vocabulary of deplorable nouns multiplied for my friends and me as news of the Electoral College vote arrived in November. How can we survive in a political climate that threatens to destroy integrity, truthfulness, and good will? How can we endure politicians who denigrate the "other"—women, migrants, refugees, people of color and sexual diversity, the poor, the downtrodden?

Searching Scripture, I surprised myself by focusing on the book of Ruth. This biblical tale involves famine, migration (even refugee status), intermarriage, death, and recovery. It features two strong women, Naomi and Ruth, facing patriarchal power. Both Moab and Judah, enemy countries in other stories, graciously receive the arrival of the "other." No restrictions are imposed; opportunities to work and rebuild life are made available. Foreigners, widows old and young, are respected; and they make their own decisions. In the process, certain men assist but do not overpower these biblical women. Ruth does not forfeit her Moabite identity, even when she remarries a prominent rich Judahite man named Boaz. Moreover, she challenges him to do his duty by her. In turn, he recognizes her as "a woman of worth" (Ruth 3:11).

> *Xenophobia, racism, sexism, misogyny, and barriers to immigration deserve no place in our national narrative.*

To you, members of the new administration and Congress, I say: Heed the story of Ruth. Xenophobia, racism, sexism, misogyny, and barriers to immigration deserve no place in our national narrative.

If biblical messages of healing and compassion fail to persuade, a parable of Jesus may help (Matthew 13:1–9; Luke 8:4–8). A sower went out to sow. Some seed fell on the path, only to be trodden by birds. Some seed fell on the rocks and withered without moisture; some fell among thorns and choked. Only the seed that fell on good soil yielded grain. In appropriating this parable, I think of the American values of "liberty and justice for all." They are "seeds" for life—regardless of race, sex, gender, class, and origin. And I ponder: As these "seeds" fall upon you, will you provide the good soil in which they can flourish? Or will you be like the path, the rocks, or the thorns? Religious voices call all of you to accountability. Fail us not.

Repentance. Righteousness. Justice. Mercy.

Dear President Trump, Vice President Pence, Members of the Trump Administration and the 115th Congress,

Quincy, Illinois, holds a special place in the history of my church, the Church of Jesus Christ of Latter-day Saints. In the winter of 1839, thousands of beleaguered Latter-day Saints crossed the Mississippi River after being expelled from Missouri on orders of the governor. Homeless and almost hopeless, they found in Quincy open doors and open arms; they experienced religious tolerance on a community-wide scale. It is little wonder that when the Latter-day Saints moved north and founded Nauvoo, Illinois, the new city council there enacted an ordinance that welcomed religionists of all persuasions.

> *I pray that . . . you see the strangers in our midst as our brothers and sisters.*

In recent months, Latter-day Saint leaders have explicitly invoked that Nauvoo sentiment in speaking up, in the words of Joseph Smith, in defense of "any other denomination who may be unpopular and too weak to defend themselves."

Readers of the Bible do not have to go very far before they realize that the God they encounter in those pages cares about the unpopular, the weak, the stranger. The notion of the "stranger" is all a matter of perspective. Ask any Latter-day Saint what the first hymn he or she learned as a child was, and chances are you'll hear, "I Am a Child of God." Latter-day Saints take literally the words of Jesus, when he told Mary that God is "my Father, and your Father" (John 20:17), and of Paul, who called God the "Father of all" (Ephesians 4:6). In this worldview, then, every person is a brother or a sister, a fellow child of a divine and universal Father. We say with the Book of Mormon, "We see that God is mindful of every people whatsoever land they may be in . . . his bowels of mercy are over all the earth" (Alma 26:37).

With deep respect for your devotion to tackling the complex issues facing the United States today, I commend to you a familiar adage that the Latter-day Saint leader Marlin Jensen cited when he addressed Utah legislators considering an immigration bill that would have profound impact on families and on "strangers." He declared: "Immigration questions are questions dealing with God's children." Then he cautioned: "Measure twice before [you] cut."

I pray that as you "measure" and "cut," you see the strangers in our midst as our brothers and sisters.

Dear President Trump, Vice President Pence, Members of the Trump Administration and the 115th Congress,

In 1918, a soldier in the United States Army named Israel Isidore Baline wrote a composition that reads: "Let us swear allegiance to a land that is free / Let us all be grateful for a land so fair." You are probably more familiar with the song's second stanza, and with the Americanized name of its author, a Jewish immigrant who fled anti-Semitic pogroms in Russia when he was a child. In 1938, Irving Berlin's famous patriotic song debuted: "God bless America, My home sweet home."

This story serves as a testament not only to the contribution immigrants have always made to this country, but to the importance of the arts. Without a doubt, the arts and humanities have played an essential role in making America great, enriching the lives of our citizens at home and enhancing the image of the U.S. abroad.

An appreciation of the value of the arts goes back to the Hebrew Bible. Genesis recounts the origins of human civilization and culture, highlighting Jubal as the ancestor of all who played the lyre and the pipe (Genesis 4:21). After crossing the sea on dry land, the prophet Miriam and the women went out with hand drums, singing and dancing to celebrate their liberation from Egypt (Exodus 15:20–21). The book of Exodus showcases the work of Bezalel, the artisan in charge of the Tabernacle who was "endowed with a divine spirit of skill, ability and knowledge in every kind of craft" (Exodus 31:3). The Bible even depicts God as a potter, as in Isaiah 64:7: "You are our Father. We are the clay, and You are the Potter. We are all the work of Your hands."

> "
> *An appreciation of the value of the arts goes back to the Hebrew Bible.*

David served as a court musician for King Saul, who "would find relief and feel better" when David played the lyre (1 Samuel 16:23). Because of his musical abilities, King David traditionally is credited with authorship of the entire book of Psalms. Still today, in almost every church and synagogue in this country, you can hear musical interpretations of the Psalms, a celebration of the power of poetry and music.

The arts are important in the Bible and matter dearly to the communities who cherish this sacred book. I call upon you to fight for continued financial support for the arts and humanities. In the words of Irving Berlin, let us "raise our voices in a solemn prayer" for the values and priorities that have defined and distinguished our country.

DAY 66, LETTER 66

Shawnee M. Daniels-Sykes

Dear President Trump, Vice President Pence, Members of the Trump Administration and the 115th Congress,

A primary principle of Catholic social teaching is human dignity, which means that *all* human beings are persons created in the image and likeness of God (Genesis 1:26–27). Therefore, as sisters and brothers, we have a special responsibility to uphold all human life with faith, hope, and love.

As a Roman Catholic theological ethicist, I believe God sent Jesus Christ to show us how to live out this remarkable responsibility. Jesus' liberating mission detailed his encountering and accompanying human beings of various backgrounds as he brought "good news" to the poor and the oppressed (Luke 4:18–19).

The campaign slogan "Make America Great Again" seems to imply a desire to unify this deeply divided country. However, this slogan misses the fact that for centuries a diverse array of people has populated this country. America is not an island in and of itself. It is inhabited by Native American Indians, descendants of African slaves, Europeans immigrants, Asians and South Pacific Islanders, Latinxs, newer immigrants, refugees, migrant workers, and a variety of professionals, students, and visitors who travel in and out of the United States.

> **The coming of the Holy Spirit at Pentecost . . . illustrates the potential for unity amidst diversity.**

The coming of the Holy Spirit at Pentecost, when "they were all together in one place" (Acts 2:1–13), illustrates the potential for unity amidst diversity. As leaders, you have a major responsibility to bring about unity, peace, and prosperity in our country and around the world. In the first few months of this new term, how are your words and actions contributing to this aim? Mean-spirited mockeries, brash statements, and defensive tweets only exploit divisions and sow hatred, violence, and fear. Harsh and divisive edicts threaten to tear apart hard-working families and keep out worthy individuals who could contribute to our country. Draconian budget proposals that eviscerate support for the needy will not make America great: they will hurt the very people who count on you to improve their lives.

As you lead this nation, what will you do to "seek the welfare" (Jeremiah 29:7) of the towns and cities you serve? What will you do to ensure that everyone in this country knows "how very good and pleasant it is when brothers and sisters live together in unity" (Psalm 133:1)?

Dear President Trump, Vice President Pence, Members of the Trump Administration and the 115th Congress,

As a Tejana from the Mexico/U.S. border, I have been formed by this community. I have seen people of faith live out their beliefs and use their community networks to attend to the ever-fluctuating needs of migrants, even when their own jobs and livelihoods are torn apart by the decisions of two distant governments.

Following your own words, Mr. Trump—"Together, we will make love and tolerance prevalent throughout the world"—I ask that you visit communities along the Mexico/U.S. border and come to know the people and their needs before making any additional decisions about this area. Listen to two wise women who spoke during Pope Francis' visit to the Mexico/U.S. border:

> *How are we keeping people and communities connected, when imprisoned or living on opposite sides of the border?*

Daisy Flores Gámez, alluding to Mark 2:21–22, declared: "We do not want our children to grow not knowing God and without minimal human capacities. For these reasons we believe we need to do something about it. Because it is in our families, factories, schools, churches and corporations, together with our governing bodies that we should attempt to build a new society as well as a new form of seeing life and relating to one another."

Evelia Quintana Molina admitted: "One day I found myself sad to be far away from my home without my daughter and family. In my interior I thought, God I accept your will (Luke 22:42). And I said, 'God, I only ask that you help me see that your plans are better than mine.'"

Reflecting on their insightful remarks, consider the following questions: How are we building better societies while attending to both new and old wineskins (Mark 2:21–22), thus establishing systems that support the full flourishing of life? In order to build better societies, how are we minimizing the need to imprison people in jails and deportation centers? How are we keeping people and communities connected, when imprisoned or living on opposite sides of the border?

As we work to improve America, may we think beyond national borders and follow Pope Francis' example. He declared, "God bless America" to Congress and in Juárez, when he waved to the "VIPs": those in detention because of their documentation status, the only ones given the honor of standing on the U.S. side of the border during the pope's visit.

Dear President Trump, Vice President Pence, Members of the Trump Administration and the 115th Congress,

One of the most important stories in the New Testament is the parable of the sheep and the goats (Matthew 25:31–46). The parable is carefully structured with two different sets of parallel statements that contrast how individuals treat the hungry, the thirsty, the stranger, the naked, the ill, and the imprisoned. The story pivots on the surprising identification of these groups with Christ: "just as you did it to one of the least of these . . . you did it to me" (25:40).

This powerful parable in Matthew inspired the famous story of Martin of Tours who met a naked person at a gate and gave half of his robe to the man, only to have a dream the next night in which Christ appeared to him in the same half garment. These stories challenge Christians today to treat strangers—be they immigrants, the homeless, the other—as if every individual was Christ.

> *These stories challenge Christians today to treat strangers—be they immigrants, the homeless, the other—as if every individual was Christ.*

Several years ago I visited a university in Puebla, Mexico. My host took me to a mountain village of three hundred people. When I had lunch with the six women who ran the village, I asked, "Where are the men?" "Near Chicago," they replied. I inquired if they resented having to do everything themselves. They let me know in no uncertain terms that they did. I asked what options young men had. They explained that young men in their village could work in the fields for $10 per day (provided there was work), attend a university (although they could only remember one who had been able to do so), or go north. As I sat and listened, I knew that I would not have worked in the fields.

I hope we as Americans will remain a country that welcomes strangers and views people from *their* vantage point, not just our own. While I speak with a Christian voice, this is a moral voice shared by people of many faiths and those without faith. People around the world are watching us. Too many rightly are critical of the lack of moral leadership in the way that we treat other human beings. Restore our image as a people of high morality who value all those who dwell on this earth.

Dear President Trump, Vice President Pence, Members of the Trump Administration and the 115th Congress,

I have been thinking about the verse: "For everyone to whom much is given, from him much will be required; and to whom much has been committed, of him they will ask the more" (Luke 12:48). Let us face facts: The United States has been given a great deal, much of it an accident of history or a result of sometimes less than honorable geopolitical strategy. Some might dare call our wealth and power a "blessing." I certainly *experience* it as such, since by chance I was born an American. I did absolutely nothing to deserve the privileged circumstances in which I find myself. Whatever caused it, America's great wealth and power—and indeed anyone's wealth and power—should be a force for good rather than evil. We should be humbled, not ashamed or boastful, by how fortunate we are.

> " America's great wealth and power—and indeed anyone's wealth and power—should be a force for good rather than evil.

On a national level, the rhetoric and actions of our leaders should be full of pragmatic generosity rather than stinginess. Yes, there are limits to how much we can permit and provide. All nations have financial and security constraints. However, as a people to whom much has been given, our limits must be informed by a mandate to benefit others. We should institute policies that come from an honest but good faith assessment of the maximum we can provide for those in need, at home and abroad, without compromising our ability to be the best agent for good that we can be.

Whether we are speaking of government budgets, corporate balance sheets, or personal wealth, pragmatic generosity means that by cheerfully sharing our blessings with others, we ultimately enrich ourselves. To reach the practical, sensible goal of magnanimity being mutually beneficial for all, Scripture suggests we nurture our capacity for humility and generosity instead of giving into our propensity for cruelty and selfishness. In policymaking and personal choices, we would do well to keep in mind this biblical maxim: "Some give generously and gain all the more . . . A generous person will be enriched" (Proverbs 11:24–25).

Dear President Trump, Vice President Pence, Members of the Trump Administration and the 115th Congress,

One year before his execution, in his speech "Beyond Vietnam: A Time to Break Silence," the Rev. Dr. Martin Luther King Jr. delivered a searing message. Like a voice crying out in the wilderness (Mark 1:3), Dr. King called his government to repentance as it blanketed Vietnam with napalm and Agent Orange, warning: "A nation that continues year after year to spend more money on military defense than on programs of social uplift is approaching spiritual death." Like Israel's prophets, Dr. King understood that earthly *shalom* (holistic harmony) results from *tzedakah* (righteousness), not from extinguishing external threats, real or imagined.

Nevertheless, in the five decades since Dr. King's exhortation, the U.S. has fortified its militaristic economy, building structures of weaponized cash to rival Babel's global ambitions (Genesis 11). Today, this towering stockpile of nuclear profit casts a long shadow over some eight hundred military bases, bombing campaigns in seven countries, and a massive incarceration and deportation apparatus. Moreover, under this towering shadow, hate crimes are rising and sexual violence is rampant, particularly against indigenous, mestiza, and African-descended women.

Mr. President, your proposed 2018 budget would amplify multiple forms of violence and proliferate the spiritual rot about which Dr. King warned. This proposed budget removes protections for domestic violence survivors, imperils ecosystems, snatches food from impoverished children, extends border walls, and beats plowshares into weapons. Implementing this militaristic scheme would cause immense personal suffering and deepen cycles of violence, especially as communities deteriorate or attempt to defend themselves from your administration's assaults.

Amid these crosses, many will bear witness to suffering while pursuing the surest path to *shalom*. Indeed, we hear this lament and resolve in the words of Langston Hughes: "America never was America to me, / And yet I swear this oath— / America will be!"

We pray for resolute faith—epitomized by spirit-filled prophets from our past like Denmark Vesey and Fannie Lou Hamer—so that we too might bear what Dietrich Bonhoeffer called "the cost of discipleship." Representatives of the people, your destinies are inescapably intertwined with our suffering neighbors, whom your parties are leaving on the roadside (Luke 10:30). Hear the prophets of this land, calling us to repentance, righteousness, and new life.

On March 8, 2017, International Women's Day, we created this graphic to highlight the contribution of the fifty-four women who wrote letters for the campaign.

RELIGIOUS VOICES: DAY 71–80

LETTER 71 | MARCH 31, 2017

Zain Abdullah

Associate Professor of Religion
and Society and Islamic Studies,
Temple University

LETTER 72 | APRIL 1, 2017

Sarah Eltantawi

Assistant Professor of Comparative
Religion and Islamic Studies,
The Evergreen State College

LETTER 73 | APRIL 2, 2017

Esther J. Hamori

Associate Professor of Hebrew Bible,
Union Theological Seminary

LETTER 74 | APRIL 3, 2017

Karoline M. Lewis

Marbury E. Anderson Chair in Biblical
Preaching, Luther Seminary

LETTER 75 | APRIL 4, 2017

Bernadette J. Brooten

Robert and Myra Kraft and Jacob
Hiatt Professor of Christian Studies, of
Women's, Gender, and Sexuality Studies,
of Classical Studies, and of Religious
Studies, Brandeis University

LETTER 76 | APRIL 5, 2017

Rita D. Sherma

Director & Associate Professor
of Hindu Studies, Mira and Ajay
Shingal Center for Dharma Studies,
Graduate Theological Union

LETTER 77 | APRIL 6, 2017

Karma Lekshe Tsomo

Professor of Theology and Religious
Studies, University of San Diego

LETTER 78 | APRIL 7, 2017

Rose Aslan

Assistant Professor of Religion and
Global Islam, California Lutheran
University

LETTER 79 | APRIL 8, 2017

Phillis I. Sheppard

Associate Professor of Religion,
Psychology, and Culture, Vanderbilt
University Divinity School

LETTER 80 | APRIL 9, 2017

Nadia Kizenko

Professor of History & Director of
Religious Studies, University at Albany

Dear President Trump, Vice President Pence, Members of the Trump Administration and the 115th Congress,

We believe America is destined for greatness. The GOP slogan "Make America Great Again" echoed the party's 1980 version, "Let's Make America Great Again." The 2004 Democratic presidential bid also suggested a return to grandeur with a motto inspired by a 1938 Langston Hughes poem, "Let America Be America Again."

Our belief that we must be better can certainly lead to greatness. But Muslim tradition teaches us that this trek to greatness is a cautionary tale, since the Arabic words for "great" and "arrogance" share the same linguistic root (*kbr*). This insight is perhaps one reason the dome of the Library of Congress depicts Islam among the civilizations that influenced our beloved nation.

> " *. . . the greatness of any nation will depend solely on how it honors others.*

Ours is a country not founded upon ancestry, but on self-evident truths that lead to civic virtue. Many are unaware that Islam began in the seventh century with a similar vision of fairness and the common good above tribal rule. While Islam recognizes human diversity as divinely ordained, the greatness of any nation will depend solely on how it honors others (Qur'an 49:13). So please join me as I offer a prayer for America and her potential for greatness:

Oh, let America be great again, but not the greatness of the ancient Greeks, who during their dark period sought a desperate, ill-fated promise that glory would rescue their dreary lives. Let America be great again, not a greatness that leads to increased suffering, but the peacemaking greatness worthy of being called "the Children of God" (Matthew 5:9).

Oh, let America be great for her abiding protection of religious freedoms, never casting an indiscriminate eye on an entire people due to a heinous few. Let America and her people be great witnesses among the nations for truth and "steadfast maintainers of justice" (Qur'an 2:143; 4:135).

Oh, let us value Muslim Americans like Muhammad Ali, whose rants about being "the Greatest" were realized by his efforts to preserve life against the threat of unjust wars, by his demands for liberation, and by his resolve to show how pursuing happiness should extend to the developing world.

So let us pray for an America that upholds the guarantees of life, liberty, and the pursuit of happiness as the over-riding measure of our greatness at home and abroad. Amen!

Dear President Trump, Vice President Pence, Members of the Trump Administration and the 115th Congress,

I write to you as a scholar of contemporary Islam who adopts the method of "dual critique" as a personal ethos and scholarly approach. Dual critique holds that scholars of Islam—and Muslims—should be willing to critique both external factors that challenge Muslim-majority communities (such as imperialism, colonialism, militarism, racism) and internal problems within Muslim-majority communities (like sectarianism, misogyny, homophobia, intolerance).

It is from this perspective that I say in all sincerity that the Trump administration's approach to Muslims is, as he might say, "a disaster." Take just one particularly troubling statement made by the chief White House strategist Steve Bannon, who called Islam "the most radical religion in the world" and warned that members of the faith had created "a fifth column here in the United States."

Taking the long view of Islamophobia in the U.S., the Trump administration is unique in its apparent zeal to cast the American Muslim population in a suspicious light and blame Islam itself as the problem. Michael Flynn, who was President Trump's first national security advisor, referred to Islam as a "political ideology," not a religion, and called Islam a "cancer."

What is the purpose of this rhetoric, and where will it lead? Muslims in the U.S. overwhelmingly reject terrorism. American Muslims are exasperated, ashamed, and embarrassed by terrorist attacks in the name of Islam. We are a thriving, assimilated community living by the Qur'anic vision of humanity: "People, We created you from a single man and a single woman, and made you into races and tribes so that you should get to know one another" (49:13).

> **. . . *view our differences as a gift, not a threat.***

The only thing the Trump administration's extremist rhetoric does is alienate the overwhelming majority of decent American Muslims, divide our country, and weaken our social bonds. This rhetoric is a smoke screen that distracts us from troublesome policies at home and abroad, such as recent air strikes in Iraq that killed over two hundred civilians.

Demagoguery, ignorance, hatred, and inaccurate stereotypes of Muslims demean our nation and do not keep us safe. I implore cooler heads in the Trump administration to rein in the dangerous and escalatory rhetoric against Islam and Muslims. Instead, learn from the Qur'an that we all derive from one source and should view our differences as a gift, not a threat.

DAY 73, LETTER 73   *Esther J. Hamori*

Dear President Trump, Vice President Pence, Members of the Trump Administration and the 115th Congress,

Jewish tradition has always valued wisdom, which is not quite the same thing as intelligence or knowledge. Wisdom is a matter of being able to discern how best to live in the world—how to treat others, how to listen and learn, how to think before speaking, how to seek advice—and then doing so.

One ancient Jewish poet wrote: "Happy is the one who does not walk in the counsel of the wicked, or stand in the path of the guilty, or sit in the seat of the scornful . . . He will be like a tree planted beside streams of water, that bears its fruit in its season, and its leaf does not wither; in all that he does he prospers" (Psalm 1:1, 3).

The first word of this psalm (*ashre*) is sometimes translated as "blessed," but it means "happy" or "fortunate." One need not be Jewish, nor religious at all, to learn from ancient wisdom about how to be happy and fortunate. The poem says:

> *Wisdom is a matter of being able to discern how best to live in the world—how to treat others, how to listen and learn, how to think before speaking, how to seek advice . . .*

- Do not look to reprehensible people for advice.
- Do not align yourself with blameworthy people.
- Do not treat others with scorn.

President Trump, to whom do you look for advice? For your chief strategist and closest advisor, you selected the anti-Semitic white nationalist ally Steve Bannon. With whom do you align yourself? For U.S. attorney general, the person to lead our nation's Justice Department, you chose Jeff Sessions, a man culpable for civil rights and voting rights injustices. How do you treat others? In your words and actions, you have scorned innumerable people, including Muslims whom you have maligned and targeted, immigrants you have demeaned and persecuted, and women whose pussies you have boasted about grabbing.

As a woman, a Jew, a scholar, a person with some hope for humanity—and as a patriot who values liberty and justice for *all* and wants the best for America—I hope you will seek out advisors with integrity, stand with honest leaders, and treat the citizens of our country and others with dignity and respect.

Dear President Trump, Vice President Pence, Members of the Trump Administration and the 115th Congress,

One of the most well known verses in the New Testament comes from John 3:16: "For God so loved the world that he gave his only son." How does that love manifest itself?

In John 4:1–42, Jesus and his disciples travel through Samaria so Jesus can show them what loving the world looks like. The "world" looks like the woman he meets at Jacob's well: a Samaritan, a foreigner, a woman ostracized from her community for having been widowed or divorced five times, likely for being barren. Not only does the Samaritan woman recognize the value of the "living water" Jesus provides (4:11–15), but many other Samaritans "believed in him because of the woman's testimony" (4:39). Although the Samaritan woman becomes an ideal witness for Jesus, her so-called sexual immorality continues to dominate her story's interpretation: She is blamed and shamed by a persistent, systemic sexualization of women.

> *Demeaning rhetoric about women and blatant misogyny jeopardize the many strides forward made by women in religious leadership.*

As a woman leader in the church, I routinely confront sexism, which churches continue to sanction. I experience firsthand, or hear from students and colleagues, the many ways women in ministry are devalued. We are told women should not be pastors. We are told the only value of our ministry is in our looks. We are told we should be silent. These claims are supported by Scripture, validated by tradition, and now seemingly justified by our current president. Yet the Samaritan woman substantiates that the Bible does not sanction the silencing of women. Our accomplishments as clergy prove that we, too, help people encounter the "living water."

Demeaning rhetoric about women and blatant misogyny jeopardize the many strides forward made by women in religious leadership. God became flesh, committing to the fullness of the incarnation for everyone, not just for half of humanity.

I urge you all to think about what your words and policies communicate about women and their value, and how that affects the women in your lives: your wives, daughters, mothers, sisters, friends, constituents. Any laws or executive orders that view women as "less than" are incongruent with the story of the woman at Jacob's well and inconsistent with the Bible's insistence that both women and men are created in God's image.

DAY 75, LETTER 75 *Bernadette J. Brooten*

Dear President Trump, Vice President Pence, Members of the Trump Administration and the 115th Congress,

Preventing discrimination based on sex, race, disability, and other protected classes is a moral issue. You can expect religious and nonreligious women and allies to resist any federal actions that would reverse the recent modest progress to address discriminatory violence.

Although Christian leaders have not always seen sexual, racial, or other forms of discriminatory violence as an important moral priority—and many today still do not—Christians increasingly do oppose such violence and work with persons from other religious traditions, as well as with agnostics and atheists, to prevent it. Recognizing the long-term economic, medical, psychological, and spiritual toll on survivors and their communities, many persist in calling for justice.

Marginalized and minoritized Christians and allies often find inspiration in the Bible. In Luke 18:1–8, Jesus tells a parable of a persistent woman who lives in a city with an unjust judge "who neither feared God nor had respect for people." The widow keeps coming to him, insisting, "Grant me justice against my opponent." After initially refusing her demands, he eventually relents: "Though I have no fear of God and no respect for anyone, yet because this widow keeps bothering me, I will grant her justice, so that she may not wear me out by continually coming." This parable comes to teach Jesus' followers "not to lose heart" and not to delay granting justice, especially for those who are vulnerable and in need of an advocate.

The same Bible tells of other persistent women. Tamar claims her legal right to bear children and is recognized as in the right for her unconventional tactics to obtain justice (Genesis 38). A Gentile woman protests when Jesus compares her to a dog, insisting that he help her daughter (Matthew 15:21–28; Mark 7:24–29). Each woman succeeds—because she persists.

> *Preventing discrimination based on sex, race, disability, and other protected classes is a moral issue.*

If the government rolls back protections for those who experience discriminatory violence, women and other people of faith will fight for justice. If the government fails to provide adequate resources to enforce federally guaranteed rights and to assist communities, schools, and workplaces in reducing harm, we will persist in demanding justice.

Rita D. Sherma

Dear President Trump, Vice President Pence, Members of the Trump Administration and the 115th Congress,

> **The dynamic determination of the American dream is to create one people out of many origins, one story from many narratives.**

The foundational principle of *E Pluribus Unum* ("Out of Many, One") is stamped on one side of the Great Seal of the United States, along with the motto *Novus Ordo Seclorum* ("New Order of the Ages") on the other side. The dynamic determination of the American dream is to create one people out of many origins, one story from many narratives. This vision of creating a nation unlike any other led us to a new order forged in freedom. This dream and this drive are emblazoned on the Great Seal and etched on the hearts and minds of trailblazing Americans of every color and creed.

Another eighteenth-century visionary document, the U.S. Bill of Rights, states in Amendment V that no person shall be deprived of life, liberty, or property without due process of law. Yet, in the first few months of the new administration, blameless Americans and legal, law-abiding residents of the United States, including those of the Hindu faith, have been shot down in cold blood by those who believe that legal American residency is the privilege of just one ethnicity, race, and religion.

In such incidents, a few violent minds have sought to overthrow the wisdom of our founders. Such efforts are motivated not by fidelity to our foundational principles, but by conformity with the purveyors of intolerance. They have failed in the past and will fail again. It will enhance the legacy of our president, his administration, and Congress if all violence against innocents is unequivocally condemned by our leaders.

These times take me back to the Upanishads, the canonical sacred scriptures of my 4,000-year-old Hindu faith, with its vast history of peaceful coexistence and resolve to forge "one out of many."

Om saha nāv avatu — May He protect us both together
saha nau bhunaktu — May He nourish us both together
saha vīryaṃ karavāvahai — May we work conjointly with great dynamism
tejasvi nāv adhītam astu — May our intellectual effort be vigorous and effective
mā vidviṣāvahai — May we not have any conflict with each other
Om śāntiḥ śāntiḥ śāntiḥ Aum! — Let there be peace, peace, peace!

Dear President Trump, Vice President Pence, Members of the Trump Administration and the 115th Congress,

As a Buddhist scholar and practitioner, I would like to share some wisdom from my religious heritage with those who have been elected to lead our nation as public servants.

Love and compassion are universal values cherished by people around the world. The Buddha taught these values as antidotes to destructive emotions and behavior. Cultivating inner peace is a powerful way to overcome anger, jealousy, pride, and selfishness. We begin by generating loving-kindness toward ourselves, and then expand these feelings to others: neighbors, colleagues, enemies, and gradually the whole world.

Shantideva (685–763), a Bengali Buddhist scholar, taught: "All happiness comes from cherishing others. All misery comes from cherishing oneself."

The *Questions of King Milinda* is a dialogue between a Buddhist monk named Nagasena and a second-century BCE Indo-Greek king named Menander (Milinda) I. The text depicts an ideal Buddhist ruler who practiced the values of nonviolence, justice, and compassion and thus created a peaceful, harmonious, prosperous society. As a consequence, naturally he was beloved by all.

> *Will you find constructive solutions to help relieve suffering in the world?*

One need not be a world leader to put this Buddhist wisdom into practice. My experience teaching meditation in U.S. prisons over the years has shown that those who are incarcerated also respond well to meditations on compassion, especially when the practice of generating compassion develops gradually, starting with oneself.

A leader who embodies these virtues will be remembered fondly for ages to come. Will you be remembered as a wise and compassionate leader? Will you find constructive solutions to help relieve suffering in the world? We hope we can count on you.

Rose Aslan

Dear President Trump, Vice President Pence, Members of the Trump Administration and the 115th Congress,

With much misinformation being spread by politicians and the media, and with growing hostility among Americans, we need healing and soul searching to find a place of balance and equanimity in our country. In the Islamic tradition, we believe that change must first come from within and that we cannot blame others for our problems. Our religion demands that we be agents of change, as God says in the Qur'an: "God does not change the condition of a people unless they change what is in themselves" (13:11). We need to go beyond stereotypes and see our fellow Americans as fellow humans. We should make it our mission to focus on what binds us together as a nation rather than what divides us.

> *We need to go beyond stereotypes and see our fellow Americans as fellow humans.*

Mr. President, your words and actions, and those of others in your administration, suggest that you view Muslims as an enemy and seek to restrict our rights as citizens and legal residents. You stoke fear among some Americans against their fellow citizens, despite the fact that Muslims have been part of the American fabric since before we became a nation in 1776 and have made significant contributions to our country.

No matter how many times you try to limit our rights and our movement, Muslims in this country will always take the high road, as God demands of us in the Qur'an: "Good and evil cannot be equal. Repel evil with what is better, and your enemy will become as close as an old and valued friend, but only those who are steadfast in patience, only those who are blessed with great righteousness, will attain to such goodness" (41:34–35).

Going forward in your service to the American people, remember that Americans from all religious traditions are counting on you to maintain our nation's values of liberty, justice, and equality for all, without exceptions. We will keep you accountable to your duty as the "leader of the free world" to uphold our Constitution and American ideals.

We should embrace each other because of our differences. This is what has made us great in the past and what holds the promise of our future. The more we affirm and contribute to building a pluralistic society, the more we will reap its potential.

DAY 79, LETTER 79

Phillis I. Sheppard

Dear President Trump, Vice President Pence, Members of the Trump Administration and the 115th Congress,

We are embroiled in a struggle for the soul of our country that may well determine our future capacity to be considered "united states."

History reveals that we have mistreated whole groups of people by creating patterns of discord and societal divides: violence against indigenous peoples by the earliest European immigrants, the betrayal of Japanese Americans during World War II, the legacy of the slave trade that haunts us daily. These exclusionary forces have rendered some members of our society nearly invisible or made them targets of physical and emotional violence or victims of unjust deportation. The prophet Jeremiah lamented: "Is there no balm in Gilead? Is there no healer?" (Jeremiah 8:22). The same question can be asked of the United States today.

> *This radical form of love and caring for others is how we are called to live our corporate life.*

As part of the upcoming Holy Week of Easter, Maundy Thursday commemorates Jesus' celebration of his last Passover. Even knowing his days were numbered, Jesus demonstrated his commitment to humanity when he washed his disciples' feet and declared: "A new commandment I give to you, that you love one another. Just as I have loved you, you should love one another" (John 13:34).

This radical form of love and caring for others is how we are called to live our corporate life. Love should be the ethic that shapes our treatment of neighbors near and far. Love should infuse our treatment of the stranger who seeks solace, hospitality, a new home. Love should fuel our drive to pursue justice for those pushed to the edges of society. Concrete, public, transformative expressions of love are the clearest reflections of our relationship with the Jesus of the Easter narrative. This is how we embody this most important lesson of the Christian faith.

In order to turn our hearts and actions in the direction of a Maundy Thursday love, we must acknowledge and confess the painful parts of our past. If not, our original sins threaten to derail us from becoming a nation that strives to provide liberty and justice for all, regardless of nationality, ethnicity, economic status, class, sexuality, religious commitment, or gender. We can be a beacon that offers hope for a more loving, just, and welcoming society—if only we imagine this future and work to bring it to fruition.

Dear President Trump, Vice President Pence, Members of the Trump Administration and the 115th Congress,

People sometimes understand dissent to mean something lofty, something courageous—a right enshrined in the very fabric of American life. America was originally a place of hope for religious dissenters. In politics, the United States came into existence as an act of protest against a distant king.

But dissent can also mean something more familiar from everyday life. In Holy Week before Easter, the Orthodox Church reads a selection from the Gospel of Matthew that includes the parable of the two sons (Matthew 21:28–32). Jesus describes how "a man had two sons, and he came to the first and said, 'Son, go, work today in my vineyard.' The first one refused, saying, 'I will not'; but afterward he regretted it and went. The second immediately agreed, saying, 'Yes, sir, I go!'; but he did not go."

This parable tells us something simple about human nature. It is often easier to agree to do something than it is to refuse. Agreeing avoids trouble in the short term. It avoids confrontation. It even leaves open the possibility of an escape hatch.

It is much harder to refuse immediately. This leaves you open to criticism and discipline. It is just as hard to rethink one's initial reaction—and to act on that reflection rather than the impulse.

Now, on one level, this parable seems to teach that actions speak louder than words. That message comes through when Jesus asks his listeners, "Which of the two did the will of his father?" and they respond, "The first" (Matthew 21:31). But the parable also suggests that neither quick dissent nor quick agreement is the virtue here. The virtue is doing the right thing.

> *. . . neither quick dissent nor quick agreement is the virtue here. The virtue is doing the right thing.*

This might be a consolation for someone in public office. If you, as leaders, said you would *not* do something, or said you *would*, the promise and the quick impulse is not what you will be judged by. If you rethink them, you need not necessarily be bound by your earlier words. Like the first son, you are free to reflect and do what really seems right.

Benjamin Brown created this illustration after reading Letter 6. Uriah Kim tells the president: "I pray that . . . you will continue to leave America's door open and care for all those already living in the United States." Letters 81–88, which appeared during the week of Passover, pick up on the themes of hospitality and welcoming the stranger.

RELIGIOUS VOICES: DAY 81–90

LETTER 81 | APRIL 10, 2017

Choon-Leong Seow
Vanderbilt, Buffington, Cupples Chair
in Divinity & Distinguished Professor
of Hebrew Bible, Vanderbilt University
Divinity School

LETTER 82 | APRIL 11, 2017

Maria Teresa Dávila
Associate Professor of Christian Ethics,
Andover Newton Theological School

LETTER 83 | APRIL 12, 2017

Ryan P. Bonfiglio
John H. Stembler Scholar in Residence,
First Presbyterian Church of Atlanta

LETTER 84 | APRIL 13, 2017

Ellen M. Ross
Howard M. and Charles F. Jenkins
Professor of Quakerism and Peace Studies
& Peace and Conflict Studies Program
Coordinator, Swarthmore College

LETTER 85 | APRIL 14, 2017

Nirinjan Kaur Khalsa
Clinical Professor Jain and Sikh Studies,
Loyola Marymount University

LETTER 86 | APRIL 15, 2017

Katherine A. Shaner
Assistant Professor of New Testament,
Wake Forest University School of Divinity

LETTER 87 | APRIL 16, 2017

Gay L. Byron
Professor of New Testament,
Howard University School of Divinity

LETTER 88 | APRIL 17, 2017

Beatrice Lawrence
Assistant Professor of Hebrew Bible,
Seattle University

LETTER 89 | APRIL 18, 2017

Kathleen Flake
Richard Lyman Bushman Professor of
Mormon Studies, University of Virginia

LETTER 90 | APRIL 19, 2017

Joseph Walser
Associate Professor of Religion,
Tufts University

Dear President Trump, Vice President Pence, Members of the Trump Administration and the 115th Congress,

America is a country of migrants and refugees. According to the Bible, Israel too was a country of migrant and refugees. That experience shaped their vision of how those who profess to love God with all their hearts (Deuteronomy 6:4) should behave.

Deuteronomy 15 specifies what such love entails, beginning with the periodic forgiveness of debt (vv. 1–6). The people are instructed: "Do not be hard-hearted or tight-fisted towards your needy compatriots . . . but open your hand and lend them whatever they need (vv. 7–8). They are to "give liberally and without a grudge" (v. 10). Moreover, when the terms of their indentured servants end, they must "not send them away empty-handed . . . but provide [for them] liberally" (vv. 13–14). The people must act liberally because they themselves had been liberated from Egypt (v. 15).

Deuteronomy 26 recounts a service of thanksgiving for a successful harvest. The worshippers bringing the first fruits of their crop would tell the story of their redemption—a story still retold every year at Passover. On the verge of perishing, they migrated to a foreign land where they were strangers and oppressed until God set them free and brought them into their new homeland (vv. 5–9). The passage ends with the charge: "You shall rejoice in all the good which the Lord your God has given to you and to your house, you and the Levite, and the stranger in your midst" (v. 11). There is no triumphalism in this liturgy, no proclamation of Israelite exceptionalism. Rather, bounty leads to shared blessings. Owning this history leads those who were once marginalized and dislocated to broaden their notion of "household" to include the Levites, who were without land, and the non-Israelite residents, who were protected and embraced.

> "
> *The people must act liberally because they themselves had been liberated from Egypt . . .*

The Bible is by no means unique in its vision of a just society. Other cultures of ancient Western Asia and Egypt shared the sense of responsibility to care for the vulnerable. Rulers were expected to act not on behalf of the rich and powerful, but for those who did not have the wherewithal to survive on their own. Those who were unwilling or unable to execute justice lost their legitimacy and were called upon to abdicate their power. Let those who govern today take heed!

Dear President Trump, Vice President Pence, Members of the Trump Administration and the 115th Congress,

Periodically I think of what the measure of my life will be. Will it be financial or professional success? Will it be a long list of academic accolades or the wealth of a large family? As often as I ask the question, the same answer enters my heart and my mind: hospitality. I pray that when I die I am measured by the welcome I offered stranger, family, foe, friend, documented, alternately documented, heterosexual or LGBTQI+. I want my legacy to be that in my home, heart, and mind, all are truly welcome.

I find the beckoning call to practice hospitality deep in my faith tradition. My life has been shaped by stories of hospitality that overturn our expectations of who is welcome and who is not: from the hospitality of Pharaoh's daughter—who by taking in Moses lifted up an entire people's freedom from the waters (Exodus 2:5–10)—to the hospitality of the woman who was judged as sinful by her townspeople but who washed Jesus' feet with her tears and her hair (Luke 7:36–50).

> *Today, as in biblical times, the greatness of a people . . . is its ability to exercise hospitality . . .*

These texts also seep into my understanding of this great nation: not only hospitality to peoples of diverse origin, but hospitality to diverse ideas and faiths. This has become the very identity of the city I live in, Malden, Massachusetts, and so many other cities and towns in the United States. Today, as in biblical times, the greatness of a people, its cities and towns, its schools and institutions, is its ability to exercise hospitality, particularly to the most vulnerable members of the human family.

In the plans this administration has presented for the welfare of the nation, I fail to see hospitality honored as a cherished trait of this nation. In the executive orders and legislative agenda for the coming months, I continually read of exclusive entry, differential treatment, and disenfranchisement for the vulnerable. I implore you all to consider how the hospitality of others has enabled you and your loved ones to be where you are today. Look to implement policies through the lens of hospitality, so that our legacy may be a national tapestry of welcome.

Dear President Trump, Vice President Pence, Members of the Trump Administration and the 115th Congress,

The command to "love thy neighbor" is at the heart of the Judeo-Christian moral code. Jesus names it as the second greatest commandment (Matthew 22:39), while the Hebrew Bible affirms that loving one's neighbor is essential to Israel being a holy people (Leviticus 19:18). Yet, who exactly *is* our neighbor?

This question is relevant for many Americans today. In our ever-diversifying demographic landscape, many of us have neighbors who look quite different than us. They were born in different countries and come from diverse cultures. They speak a range of languages and eat unfamiliar foods. Some worship in churches or synagogues, others in temples or mosques. These individuals might live next door, but are they truly our neighbors? Ought we to love them in the same way as we love those neighbors who look, speak, eat, and worship like us?

> " *. . . who exactly is our neighbor?*

We find an answer to this pressing question in Leviticus 19:34, part of the "Holiness Code." This verse calls on the Israelites not only to love their neighbors, but also to love the *strangers* in their midst, "for you were strangers in the land of Egypt." The Hebrew term for stranger, *ger*, refers to those who have come from outside of the land to stay within the Israelite community. In the ancient world, the *ger* would have faced an uncertain existence. Lacking certain rights and privileges, they could easily be driven into the margins of society, left economically, socially, and politically vulnerable. Yet every major law code in the Hebrew Bible shows compassionate concern for the welfare of the *ger*, often with a command not to wrong or oppress the *ger* (Exodus 22:20; 23:9; Deuteronomy 27:19). Leviticus 19:34 goes further, insisting the people of Israel must treat strangers as neighbors—"The stranger who resides with you shall be to you as one of your citizens"—and love both groups "as yourself."

I hope and pray that as you serve as leaders of this nation, you will honor this radical ethic of love for neighbor and stranger in your words, actions, and policies. In doing so, you will not only fulfill a commandment that is dear to many Americans, but you will help us become a stronger, freer, and more just nation.

Dear President Trump, Vice President Pence, Members of the Trump Administration and the 115th Congress,

As leaders of our nation, I imagine you seek to bring all Americans together to build a better future. Quaker voices offer insight to those of us working to achieve that goal.

Philadelphia Quaker leader Anthony Benezet (1713–1784) observed that humans have an inborn affinity for one another. Sharing a common humanity, we are all a part of "one family." For Christians, the fundamental commandment that humans should love one another (John 13:34–35) affirms this inborn affinity.

Still, Benezet knew, if we turn away from one another, we live in constant danger of falling prey to what he regarded as the greatest calamity that can befall humanity: "hardness of heart."

> *. . . the antidote to hardness of heart is the cultivation of compassion . . .*

He pondered how we who regard ourselves as "generous and humane" could treat other humans cruelly, "without a feeling of great remorse."

Now is the time to hear Benezet's challenge and consider how we diminish ourselves when we act in repressive and warlike ways. When not only individuals, but also nations, "grow gradually from bad to worse, they, at the same time, become more and more hardened." As a result, they become "reconciled to practices for which they had at first the utmost detestation and abhorrence."

The preeminent American Quaker reformer Lucretia Mott (1793–1880)—whose image will soon be on the $10 bill—noticed how often we silence our own awareness of the injustices surrounding us. "I believe it is high time there was more . . . moral courage," she wrote. As we are implicated in the harming of others, whether by our actions or by turning our eyes away from the suffering we perceive, we become increasingly alienated from ourselves and from the communities around us, more deeply mired in the sicknesses of the world.

For Benezet and Mott, the antidote to hardness of heart is the cultivation of compassion. They urge us to listen to the still, small voice within. Tenacious and persevering, this voice reminds us of times when we have felt compassion for others. By remembering our common humanity, we sow the seeds of transformation and contribute to the realization of a better future for all people.

Dear President Trump, Vice President Pence, Members of the Trump Administration and the 115th Congress,

"If you can't see God in All, you can't see God at all." As Sikhs, we are taught to serve others selflessly because in doing so we serve the divine that shines through all life. Sikhism, the fifth largest religion, was founded in India in the early 1500s by Guru Nanak, who proclaimed that humanity is One and that we are all equal regardless of class, faith, gender, or ethnicity. This recognition gives us the responsibility to act, think, and speak ethically in our daily lives.

As a second-generation Anglo-American Sikh who is descended from Protestant clergy and teaches at a Jesuit university, I question the ethics of an administration whose separatist ideologies have energized hate rhetoric and violence. Since the election, there has been an escalation of hate crimes, particularly aimed at Sikhs. Identified by turbans and beards, to an unknowing public Sikhs visually represent terrorism, fear, and distrust. Quite the opposite, these physical articles of faith are meant to signify a Sikh's willingness to stand against injustice and defend the freedom and equality of all.

> *As Sikhs, we are taught to serve others selflessly because in doing so we serve the divine that shines through all life.*

The turbaned Sikh identity was given by the tenth Sikh Guru, Guru Gobind Singh, after his father, the ninth Sikh Guru, refused to be converted by a tyrannical power and gave his own life for the religious freedom of All. During the spring celebration of Baisakhi in April 1699, Guru Gobind Singh instructed the Sikhs not to hide, but to don the turban as warrior saints who have pride in their faith and fearlessly stand for the rights of all. Guru Gobind Singh proclaimed: "I'm telling the truth, listen everyone! The ones who have mastered the art of universal love, are the ones who find God" (Akal Ustat).

May we have the courage to stand united in love as one nation, under God, so that America truly may be the land of the free and home of the brave. As an American Sikh I pray:

May the long time sun shine upon you
All love surround you
And the pure light within you
Guide your way on
Sat Nam

Dear President Trump, Vice President Pence, Members of the Trump Administration and the 115th Congress,

Over the past few years Black Lives Matter, Say Her Name, Mothers of the Movement, and other grassroots organizations have reminded us that America's legacy of violence against black and brown people is a plague on our civil body politic. If America is to be a just society, denying this disease is unacceptable.

My work in New Testament studies recognizes this disease in the Roman Empire. Then, as now, race-based, state-sanctioned violence was a common occurrence. Those who ran the Roman Empire erected stone monuments carved with images celebrating the empire's power over the people it had enslaved. In these images, Roman emperors hold female figures by the hair, exposing anguished faces and twisted bodies. The emperors are depicted god-like in their triumph, exercising bald power over their enemies, who, paradoxically, are portrayed as both dangerous criminals and weak, pathetic losers. These carvings would have been considered "patriotic" in their day.

> *Domination, conquest, exploitation . . . are antithetical to divine power.*

Some early Christians explicitly rejected such grotesque celebrations of power. A poem about Jesus in Philippians 2:5–11 describes what true divine power entails. The poem celebrates Jesus Christ as one who is in the form of God and is equal to God (v. 6). Contrary to what the Roman rulers thought, the poem states clearly that divine power does not include the right to dominate and subdue other people. Jesus became like the women in the Roman reliefs (vv. 6–8): He took the form of a slave, and he was executed as a criminal. Domination, conquest, exploitation—exactly the "patriotic" images that the Roman Empire embraced—are antithetical to divine power.

My Christian faith holds that Jesus' death and resurrection reject our human displays of power and violence. Violence, fear, and death are not God's plan; and they should not be part of America's plan either. Leaders who glorify dominance over other people, who criminalize black and brown bodies, who objectify women, and who exploit poverty work against God's justice.

Gay L. Byron

Dear President Trump, Vice President Pence, Members of the Trump Administration and the 115th Congress,

On January 20, 2017, while you were assuming your new leadership positions, I was commemorating what would have been my biological father's 100th birthday. I remembered the life of the man who first taught me to read the Bible, who first demonstrated the importance of civic engagement and advocacy, and who modeled what it means to keep the faith despite the circumstances.

I write this letter in memory not only of my father, but also the great cloud of witnesses (Hebrews 11:1–40; 12:1–3) who endured slavery and various manifestations of Jim Crow, who built the White House you now claim as home, who educated their children by making a way out of no way, who lived in substandard housing and labored in inequitable employment situations, who—despite all of this—dreamed dreams, overturned unjust laws, and lived to tell their stories.

> "
>
> *The resurrection stories and the miracle of the empty tomb bear witness to the fact that death is not the final word, that light triumphs over darkness . . .*

I likewise write this letter because I am troubled by the example we are setting for our children. This experiment called "democracy" is looking like a farce. If "we the people" sit back and allow this unprecedented display of governance to unfold as if "business as usual," then we just may witness the premature death of our nation and its great potential as "the land of the free and the home of the brave."

The resurrection stories and the miracle of the empty tomb bear witness to the fact that death is not the final word, that light triumphs over darkness, and that life extends beyond the grave. The Gospels record different versions of the story: Some were weeping and afraid when Jesus was crucified and buried (Matthew 28:4; Mark 16:8), while others did not lose heart (Matthew 28:5–8; Mark 16:9–10). They garnered courage and resolve to move forward, take action, and proclaim "the good news to the whole creation" (Matthew 28:1–8; Mark 16:15).

On this Easter, I hope you will find time to reflect on the mystery of the cross, the meaning of the resurrection, and the enduring power of God's grace and mercy. May you be encouraged to take stock of your early actions and ponder the words of Psalm 139: "Search me, O God, and know my heart . . . See if there is any wicked way in me, and lead me in the way everlasting" (vv. 23–24). Keep the faith.

Dear President Trump, Vice President Pence, Members of the Trump Administration and the 115th Congress,

The Bible's deep concern for strangers is well known, as is the need to treat them with kindness and justice (for instance, Exodus 22:20–21; Leviticus 19:33–-34; Jeremiah 7:6). The repeated command to protect the stranger emerges from the Israelites' own experience of oppression in Egypt and from the expectation that the memory of suffering must breed compassion and a passion for justice.

The book of Leviticus takes this notion of Israel's identification with the stranger even further. In the laws of the Jubilee, we read that once every fifty years, all land must be returned to its original owners. This requirement certainly has an economic element, but its primary purpose is ethical: to prevent the rich from exploiting the poor and to avoid the pain of permanent displacement. God explains why: "For the land is mine; you are but strangers and sojourners with me" (Leviticus 25:23). The land is not ours; we are but temporary residents on this earth—strangers and sojourners each and every one of us.

> *The land is not ours; we are but temporary residents on this earth—strangers and sojourners each and every one of us.*

As part of the Jubilee laws, we find a verse that plays a prominent role in U.S. history and our self-image as a nation: "You shall proclaim liberty throughout the land to all its inhabitants" (Leviticus 25:10). In 1751, the Pennsylvania Assembly selected this verse to be engraved on a bell ordered to commemorate the fiftieth year of the Pennsylvania "Charter of Privileges." The word translated as "liberty" (*dror*) here and on the "Liberty Bell" actually means "release" in its biblical context. This verse articulates the goal of the Jubilee: to ensure freedom from lifelong debt and economic oppression. The demand to release persons and land periodically "was a reminder that liberty comes from God, the true owner of all property" (Daniel Dreisbach, *Reading the Bible with the Founding Fathers*).

Thus, we cannot allow ourselves to pretend that any of us *own* this country. We must remember that we are merely borrowing the earth from its Creator, who has bestowed upon us the task of caring for the land and its people. In order to fulfill this obligation, we must heed the divine command: "Justice, justice you shall pursue" (Deuteronomy 16:20).

Dear President Trump, Vice President Pence, Members of the Trump Administration and the 115th Congress,

It is often stated as a self-sufficient fact that "without justice there is no peace." But justice alone is insufficient: peace requires mercy. Many of the ideas promoted and actions taken by the current government have been merciless. They not only threaten to harm individuals, but the nation at home and abroad.

It is well known that the Church of Jesus Christ of Latter-day Saints has added new scripture to the Bible, including the Book of Mormon, the source of the Church's nickname. The book belies the Mormons' reputation for optimism by being an extended eulogy for an ancient American people whose eventual extinction is due in no small part to their mercilessness. True or not as divine word, the book contains a warning and wisdom for us today.

> **Meant as a cautionary tale, the Book of Mormon demands generosity.**

Meant as a cautionary tale, the Book of Mormon demands generosity: "If God, who has created you . . . doth grant unto you whatsoever ye ask that is right . . . O then, how ye ought to impart of the substance that ye have one to another" (Mosiah 4:21). The book predicts dire consequences for the person who withholds mercy out of a sense of moral superiority. It describes an individual who decides not to give to the needy because he thinks the person in need "has brought upon himself his misery." Beware, the book declares, if you judge and condemn the destitute, "how much more just will be your condemnation for withholding your substance." According to the story, the counsel fell on deaf ears and, as prophesied, the miserly moralizers' substance perished with them (Mosiah 4:17, 21–23).

America is a wealthy nation by any measure, notwithstanding its debt, which is largely in service to its capitalist philosophy and strategies. Among your choices in the months ahead is how to spend that wealth and, in doing so, how to balance the nation's moral defenses with its military defenses. I ask you not to neglect the first in service to the second. I ask you to be both just and merciful, if you would have peace.

May God—of whatever definition or tradition—bless America and bless you to choose mercy and generosity.

Dear President Trump, Vice President Pence, Members of the Trump Administration and the 115th Congress,

In the aftermath of World War II, "all members of the human family" came together to draft the Universal Declaration of Human Rights. This historic document contains significant contributions by Peng Chun Chang, a Chinese scholar of Confucianism whose influence can be seen in the preamble, which states: "Disregard and contempt for human rights have resulted in barbarous acts which have outraged the conscience of mankind." The phrase "conscience of mankind" reflects the Confucian concept of the "humaneness" (*ren*) innate in all people.

> *The king possessed a modicum of goodness and righteousness; but . . . he would need to extend his compassion to all people in his realm.*

This concept appears in the story of the king of Qi, who asked Mencius, a fourth-century BCE Confucian philosopher, "What is necessary to be king?" Mencius replied that if a king protects his people, his humaneness would make them unwilling to oppose him. Mencius assured the king that he was capable of being a good ruler. How did Mencius know this? Earlier the king had seen an ox being led to sacrifice and noticed the animal trembling. Feeling compassion for the ox, he ordered the ox spared and a sheep offered instead. People criticized the king, saying he was being cheap by offering an animal of lesser value. Only Mencius realized the king had noticed the ox's suffering and spared his life out of a sense of genuine compassion. Yet Mencius also recognized the king did not see the sheep in the same way he saw the ox, just as the king was not adequately attuned to his people's suffering. The king possessed a modicum of goodness and righteousness; but to protect his kingdom and be a good king, he would need to extend his compassion to all people in his realm.

Most political leaders go into public service because they care about people and pressing issues; so they can feel hurt when others do not see the goodness of their intentions. Political failure and injustice are not necessarily due to one's heart being in the wrong place, but can result from not extending the principle of compassion far enough. Mr. Trump won the election in part because he saw the suffering of many Americans. To govern effectively, his administration needs to extend that vision so that they really see the lived experiences of all those in America.

This illustration by Brielle Gall symbolizes our efforts to capture religious voices from across the United States. From east to west, our authors hail from twenty-two states and the District of Columbia.

RELIGIOUS VOICES: DAY 91–100

LETTER 91 | APRIL 20, 2017

Tazim R. Kassam
Associate Professor of Religion,
Syracuse University

LETTER 92 | APRIL 21, 2017

Homayra Ziad
Lecturer in Islamic Studies, Johns Hopkins
University

LETTER 93 | APRIL 22, 2017

Forrest Clingerman
Professor of Religion and Philosophy,
Ohio Northern University

LETTER 94 | APRIL 23, 2017

Zayn Kassam
John Knox McLean Professor of Religious
Studies, Pomona College

LETTER 95 | APRIL 24, 2017

Love L. Sechrest
Dean of Faculty & Vice President of
Academic Affairs, Columbia Theological
Seminary

LETTER 96 | APRIL 25, 2017

Debra Majeed
Professor of Religious Studies,
Beloit College

LETTER 97 | APRIL 26, 2017

Shai Held
President and Dean, Hadar Institute

LETTER 98 | APRIL 27, 2017

Adnan Zulfiqar
Assistant Professor of Law,
Rutgers Law School

LETTER 99 | APRIL 28, 2017

Herbert R. Marbury
Associate Professor of Hebrew Bible,
Vanderbilt University Divinity School

LETTER 100 | APRIL 29, 2017

Elsie R. Stern
Vice President for Academic Affairs
& Associate Professor of Bible,
Reconstructionist Rabbinical College

Dear President Trump, Vice President Pence, Members of the Trump Administration and the 115th Congress,

To be human and humane is a high calling.

What has made America great is its humanistic spirit of tolerance and fairness, its search for individual happiness and the common good, its embrace of universal values that promise a life of liberty and security for all people, its unending hope and big-heartedness. This ethos, so beautifully expressed in the Constitution of the United States, has inspired a democracy that has won the admiration of countries all over the world. However, unless each generation of Americans—leaders and citizens alike—embodies these values and lives up to this higher calling, the unique distinction and influence of this great nation will not endure.

> *. . . unless each generation of Americans . . . lives up to this higher calling, the unique distinction and influence of this great nation will not endure.*

As a Muslim American, I hold dear the ethical principles and universal ideals of goodness and charity shared by all religions and articulated in the Qur'an. In Al-Fateha ("the Opening"), the first and most frequently recited chapter of the Qur'an (1:1–7), believers entreat God, addressed as Compassionate (*Rahman*) and Merciful (*Rahim*): "Guide us upon the straight path" (1:6). The key phrase is *sirat al-mustaqeem*, a straight, steadfast, and secure path to the common good anchored in ordinary daily conduct.

There is nothing particularly complex in this call for rectitude. Adhering to values like decency and honesty does not require subscription to a specific dogma. These principles are not the purview of a particular religion, race, gender, or political orientation. The Qur'an affirms that God bestows gifts upon every human being, "man or woman, who does righteous deeds" (16:97). Righteous conduct transcends religious identity: "Indeed, those who have attained faith, the Jews, Christians and Sabians . . . whose deeds are pure, their reward is with their Sustainer" (2:62).

Americans have long embodied this humanistic spirit, showing that life is made precious not by what we take but by what we give to each other. In this fractious time so fraught with falsehoods, we need leaders who practice these values and live lives of integrity. As elected officials in whom we have placed our trust, which path will you take to fulfill this higher calling?

Dear President Trump, Vice President Pence, Members of the Trump Administration and the 115th Congress,

A group of disciples went to the Prophet Muhammad (upon him, peace) and complained about another disciple, who they thought indulged too often in laughter. "You may be surprised to know," the Prophet replied, "that he will laugh all the way to heaven!" The message was clear: Good humor is integral to a healthy sense of self, especially for those in leadership positions.

Today's leaders can learn from the Prophet Muhammad, who was said to be among the most joyful of men, often laughing so hard that his back teeth could be seen. Muslims know well the story of the Prophet down on his hands and knees with his two precious grandsons, pretending to be a camel as they bounced on his back with glee. Disciples say they never encountered the Prophet without a smile on his face. Canonical *hadith* collections offer chapters that explicitly focus on the Prophet's laughter and good cheer as a virtue to be emulated.

> **When we learn to laugh at ourselves, and with others, we grow together in mercy and empathy.**

The Prophet understood humor as humility. He joked, bantered, and sat at ease with his disciples, drawing them close in love. He adored children, smearing their faces with food, splashing them with bathwater, kissing their tummies. He even enjoyed a good practical joke. Once a disciple secretly loosened the Prophet's saddle. When the Prophet climbed on his camel, he slipped right off—and dissolved in appreciative laughter!

We single out people who "can't take a joke" because we wonder: If they cannot laugh at themselves, can they show mercy to others? Humor helps us to not take ourselves so seriously, so we may face the slings and arrows of outrageous fortune with a light heart. Humor honors the interplay of the comic and tragic that is the subtext of our lives, helping us live with dignity by embracing the undignified. When we learn to laugh at ourselves, and with others, we grow together in mercy and empathy.

This is what we need today: leaders who exhibit mercy, empathy, and a sense of humor, leaders who are not afraid to embrace their humanity—and in so doing, embrace humankind.

Dear President Trump, Vice President Pence, Members of the Trump Administration and the 115th Congress,

Greetings on Earth Day! From its start in 1970, Earth Day has drawn the support of people from all walks of life and every corner of the country. Earth Day is also a time to remember just how closely related environmentalism and religious commitment have been in American history, as John Muir exemplifies. The beauty and fecundity of the landscape we call home is engrained in our national consciousness and celebrated as God's glorious "handiwork" (Psalm 19:2). From sea to shining sea, from the Berkshires to the Sierras, from the Great Black Swamp of my part of Ohio to Washington's Potomac watershed, our natural world is considered a blessing. We are living in a wonderful and divine Book of Nature.

Yet our economy and politics are laying siege to the environment. These are not problems affecting somewhere else, at some other time. Environmental crises are happening here and now, disproportionately affecting the most vulnerable members of our society. Our actions do violence against our human and nonhuman neighbors and threaten the entire divinely ordered cosmos.

Nowhere is this more apparent than when we reflect on U.S. climate policy. We are decades past debating the reality of climate change, yet you appointed Scott Pruitt as EPA Director, a person who has ignored the science of climate change. Furthermore, your administration proposed funding cuts for scientific monitoring and environmental research, and you have cut curbs aimed at reducing greenhouse gas emissions. Assessments like the EPA's *Climate Change Indicators in the United States* (2016) show how climate change is already affecting health, safety, the environment, and the economy. Denial of this reality is neither intellectually nor ethically acceptable.

> **On Earth Day, let us vow to mend our ways and atone for our climate sins.**

Trust in God requires us to face the truth, however terrifying or inopportune it may be to our plans and our politics. Faith in God means living in hope, working toward what theologian David Klemm and ethicist William Schweiker call "the integrity of life before God" (*Religion and the Human Future*, 2008). On Earth Day, let us vow to mend our ways and atone for our climate sins. With a sense of hope, let us take seriously our role as stewards of a world once deemed "very good" (Genesis 1:31).

Dear President Trump, Vice President Pence, Members of the Trump Administration and the 115th Congress,

As I sit here sipping my morning cup of joe, I wonder what millions of Americans who join me in that daily ritual would do if Yemenis had not figured out how to grind coffee beans and turn them into the drink we enjoy each morning. It does not matter what your religion, skin color, or culture is: The capacity within each human being for discovery and moving civilization forward is immense.

That, to me, is the promise of America: a country that provides an environment in which each person can flourish and actualize our potential to contribute to the greater good. I find this promise in the U.S. Constitution ("We the People of the United States . . . promote the general Welfare") and the Qur'an ("Allah loves those who do good"; 3:134). How will you help us fulfill this promise?

> **The capacity within each human being for discovery and moving civilization forward is immense.**

In order for individual Americans and our nation as a whole to thrive, we need a healthy natural environment. Take the humble bee, for example, about which God says in the Qur'an: "There emerges from their bellies a drink, varying in colors, in which there is healing for people" (16:69). Yet bees in America today are facing colony collapse because of neonicotinoids in pesticides, thus threatening our ability to produce food.

Will your administration be able to provide a healthy natural environment? Or will you be remembered for bringing Earth a little closer to the fires of Hell? There is no question that greenhouse gases produced by fossil fuels are accelerating the process of a hotter climate. Yet you are leasing public lands to revive the coal industry, removing emission standards, encouraging fracking, and doing your utmost to get America off clean power. What will these decisions cost Americans, now and in the future?

Nevertheless, your administration could provide visionary leadership by investing in renewable energy and upgraded electricity grids. This would produce economic and environmental benefits, put Americans back to work, and reduce our reliance on dirty oil. That way, "the righteous will be amid gardens and rivers" (Qur'an 54:54); and each person "shall sit under his vine and his fig tree, and none shall make him afraid" (Micah 4:4). Will you make it so?

Dear President Trump, Vice President Pence, Members of the Trump Administration and the 115th Congress,

A cloud hangs over our nation, and the darkness is gathering. With callous indifference, the attempted repeal of the Affordable Care Act would have denied thirty-two million people access to health care. The rollback of climate policies aimed to move us closer to a sustainable future threaten the health of the planet. Instead of challenging policies that inhibit participation in our democracy, the Justice Department has withdrawn from oversight of officials who have trampled on citizens' constitutional rights. Deportations and the travel ban have disrupted the lives of many people living here peacefully and diligently contributing to the common good.

> *. . . I urge you to adopt a humble other-regard that promotes the wholeness of the whole community.*

We have recently concluded the forty days of Lent preceding Easter. While this holy season is set aside for reflection on a dark and tragic past, this period also holds in suspense hope for liberation, freedom, and joy. Lent is a time to repent of selfishness, fear, and anger as a way of creating space for redemption, holiness, and new life.

In the epistle to the Philippians, the apostle Paul writes a letter while languishing in prison, separated from his community and disheartened by the selfish ambition and violent rivalries of enemies who do nothing but worship their own appetites. Yet even in the midst of his own darkness, the apostle calls the community to humility, service, and solidarity with the other. Exhorting his readers to imitate the extreme and generous regard for others exhibited by Jesus, Paul tells his readers to serve the interests of their neighbors: "In humility regard others as better than yourselves" (Philippians 2:3). He calls us to the joy of service to the other that anticipates the life-giving reward of service to the common good. He beckons us into the light of a life lived in service of ultimate things.

In keeping with these values, I ask you to set down the divisive politics of grievance that seek to reserve life, liberty, and the pursuit of happiness for some while withholding them from others. In keeping with the message of Paul's epistle to the Philippians, I urge you to adopt a humble other-regard that promotes the wholeness of the whole community.

Dear President Trump, Vice President Pence, Members of the Trump Administration and the 115th Congress,

Like many Americans, I embody multiple identities: I am an American of African ancestry, and I am unapologetically and unashamedly Muslim. Unlike many Americans, however, I often encounter questions as to whether these multiple identities can coexist. Especially during the most recent presidential election and the early months of the Trump administration, doubts have been raised as to whether Islam affords the level of patriotism that other Americans expect and embody.

Let me share a few facts and dispel those doubts. Muslim Americans represent more than a million registered voters and contribute to virtually all aspects of American society. As many people have discovered during "Ask A Muslim" events held throughout the country, Muslim Americans are vibrant and diverse neighbors. We are politicians—like Congressman Keith Ellison of Minnesota. We are judges—like Halim Dhanidina of California. We are law enforcement officers—like Fadia Odeh with U.S. Customs and Border Protection. We are chaplains—like Army Lt. Col. Khallid Shabazz. We are Olympians—like gold medalist Dalilah Muhammad. We are high school teachers—like Mairah Teli of Georgia. We are architects—like Virginia-based Najah Abdalla. We are entrepreneurs—

> *We are part of . . . the glorious diversity that makes our country great.*

like the Halal Guys of Manhattan. We are professional athletes—like Kenneth Faried of the Denver Nuggets. In other words, we are America.

Among the distinctive mandates of the Qur'an, the highest textual authority in Islam, is this: "O you who believe, obey God and obey the messenger and also those in charge among you" (4:59). This verse directs Muslims to follow the laws of the region in which they reside. For Muslim Americans, the practice of our religion and the responsibilities of citizenship are not incompatible.

Get to know us, not the monolithic misconceptions that drive current policies like the Muslim ban and fuel Islamophobia, anti-Muslim hate groups, and vandalism against mosques. We are part of a vast and global tapestry that is at least 1.3 billion strong and part of the glorious diversity that makes our country great. As one young Muslim proclaimed recently, "We're not going to allow any policy or federal piece of legislation to separate us and isolate us"—either as Muslims or as Americans.

Dear President Trump, Vice President Pence, Members of the Trump Administration and the 115th Congress,

The Bible begins with an amazing story about a God who speaks. Through the power of words, God creates life and confers blessing (Genesis 1). The book of Proverbs teaches: "Death and life are in the power of the tongue" (Proverbs 18:21). Like God, we can bring blessing to the world through speech that is gentle, kind, and affirming of the dignity of others. But we can also bring devastation through speech that is bitter, cruel, and degrading of others. That choice always lies before us.

> " *Like God, we can bring blessing to the world through speech . . . But we can also bring devastation . . .*

We saw this play out on the campaign trail, with crude and vulgar language becoming the norm: Mexican immigrants demeaned, the heroism of a prisoner of war belittled, women derided and debased. Now that you have the honor of serving as our nation's president, I implore you to fundamentally reorient the way you speak, so that your words can give life rather than death.

Our country was founded on a recognition of the power of speech, as evidenced in the First Amendment and our long history of zealously guarding freedom of expression. The Talmud teaches that the tongue is like the hand: both can kill (Babylonian Talmud Arakhin 15b). Some sages go further and insist that the tongue is even deadlier than the hand, because the hand can only kill those in close proximity to it, but the tongue can kill even those far away.

As our nation's leaders, you have the power to elicit people's best impulses or to stir their basest hatreds. Everything you say will reverberate and have real-life implications for millions of people. That is an immense privilege, but also an awesome responsibility. So I urge you, in the language of the Bible, to "guard your lips from speaking evil" (Psalm 34:14).

Words may create worlds, as Rabbi Abraham Joshua Heschel insisted, but they can just as surely destroy them. May you find the wisdom and the goodness to speak in ways that are worthy of your office and our nation's trust.

Dear Mr. President, Vice President Pence, Members of the Trump Administration and the 115th Congress,

American democracy relies on three branches to provide essential checks and balances: the judiciary, legislature, and executive. While there is no doubt that this separation of powers sustains our nation, it is our people who have consistently endeavored to correct our country's deepest flaws. We are the guardians of our most precious asset: dissent.

Dissent is indigenous to this land; it precedes the founding of our union. Dissenting voices have rejected enslavement, marched for rights, protested injustice, and rallied against war. They have poignantly asked, "How hypocritical is liberty?" (Tupac Shakur) and proclaimed, "Sí se puede!" (Cesar Chavez). In theory, the legislature represents the popular will; but, in essence, the people act as our fourth branch.

> *. . . dissenting voices . . . sing the melody of righteous opposition, crafted at the margins of society, in pursuit of a more moral existence.*

In fact, these dissenting voices are part of a longer tradition of raising a mirror to those in power. Many religious traditions began with dissent, and from rejected stones they became the new cornerstones (Psalm 118:22). In Islamic tradition, these voices offer *nasiha* or "sincere advice" towards a better path (Sahih al-Muslim 1:103). They sing the melody of righteous opposition, crafted at the margins of society, in pursuit of a more moral existence. In truth, they speak with a prophetic voice.

I urge you, as leaders of the nation, to listen to today's sages. Heed the counsel of the people. Know that their dissent is part of our collective story. Remember that history is not kind to obstinate leaders. Many a pharaoh has neglected the Moses in their midst. This may mean following an unpopular path, one that may diverge from party, but not from conscience. The Qur'an reminds us that to stand for justice may require "standing against oneself" (4:135).

To hear the people, you must "walk the earth with humility" (Qur'an 25:63). Recognize your limitations while endeavoring to fulfill your responsibilities. Listen most for the dissenting voices farthest away from the seats of power. Take care not to wrong them. Whether you hear them or not, the prayers of the oppressed are powerful. There is no barrier between them and God (Sahih al-Bukhari 46:9).

Dear President Trump, Vice President Pence, Members of the Trump Administration and the 115th Congress,

At the climax of the Bible's iconic parable of wanton abuse of power, corruption, and destructive self-indulgence, the prophet Nathan indicts King David: "You are the man!" (2 Samuel 12:7). Nathan rebukes the king who ordered a soldier's wife—a woman with no legal agency in the face of royal power—brought to the palace for his own pleasure and then ordered the soldier killed to hide his actions. This story of a ruler who fails to recognize his own wrongs resonates with us on multiple levels, especially with a president whose own candidacy was marred by self-indicting claims of sexual assault.

> *Nathan's call for accountability at the highest level of government speaks just as poignantly today.*

The story pricks our national moral conscience about the ways we treat foreigners in our midst, since the soldier Uriah was a Hittite, but loyal to David's kingdom. Today, our walls and policies undermine the sanctity of immigrants and their families who, like Uriah, have proven loyal to their adopted nations and often have sacrificed more than their leaders—a tragic irony in a nation of native peoples, immigrants, their descendants, and the descendants of those who were enslaved and brought here by force. Their hands and their blood have defended the civil foundation on which you stand and built the house from which you govern.

Nathan's call for accountability at the highest level of government speaks just as poignantly today. However, Nathan's statement does more than convict: It gestures toward the opportunity to be otherwise. You do not have to be "the man" whom Nathan indicts.

Become the man who keeps his promise to "cover everybody" with health care "better than Obamacare." Become the man who creates real family-sustaining jobs for the millions who pinned their hopes on each vote for you. Become the man who ensures that the Justice Department protects the lives of its black, brown, and poor citizens as zealously as it protects others.

You are not yet consigned to Nathan's pronouncement. Decide to transcend the trap of divisive nationalism and its lure toward short-term political gain. Become the president who transforms our nation and our world for the common and lasting good. The choice is yours. It is your legacy at stake. Know that however you choose, we and our children will remember. Either way, "You are the man!"

Dear President Trump, Vice President Pence, Members of the Trump Administration and the 115th Congress,

Today is the 100th day of the Trump administration. In Jewish tradition, today is also the eighteenth day of the Counting of the Omer: the 49-day period that stretches from Passover to Shavuot (Pentecost) and reminds us of the uncertain trek from liberation at the Red Sea to revelation at Mount Sinai. Like these first hundred days, the Counting of the Omer is a time of uncertainty, newness, and high expectations. Some contemporary Jews use the omer to focus our attention, one day at a time, on the attributes that we share with God—attributes that enable us, as individuals and communities, to live up to our highest potential and to move toward our highest and holiest aspirations.

> *In our diversity, we agree that these are the American values that must guide us as a nation.*

In essence, this has been the aim of the 100 letters we have sent you over these past 100 days. We have called you to enact in your leadership the crucial American values that are our greatest strength as a nation. The American Values, Religious Voices letter writers provide a snapshot of the America that you have pledged to serve. We are men and women, from red states and blue states. We identify as African American, Asian, Latinx, Native American, and white. We are Buddhists, Christians of varied denominations, Hindus, Jews, Muslims, and Sikhs. Some of our families have been in this country since before it was "America"; others are immigrants ourselves.

Yet, despite this diversity, our letters call attention to the same values: justice, compassion, protection of the vulnerable, hospitality, equal rights, and respect for all people, regardless of gender, race, religion, or status. Our writers have prayed that you will govern with wisdom and humility, putting the common good above individual concerns. In our diversity, we agree that these are the American values that must guide us as a nation.

After this 100th day, we Americans will stop counting and the American Values, Religious Voices letters will end. While the letters and the counting conclude, the call to account will continue. We writers, our readers, and millions of Americans like us insist that you preserve and promote the values that, since our founding, have grounded the American potential for greatness.

Our country's national motto, e pluribus unum, *which means
"out of many, one" (see Letters 2 and 76), captures the spirit of a campaign
designed to raise 100 voices to speak religious truth to political power.*

A READER'S RECOLLECTION

By Lia C. Howard

Executive Director, Philadelphia Commons Institute
Assistant Professor of Political Science and Liberal Studies, Templeton Honors College

In January 2017, as Donald Trump took office, I started teaching a political science course entitled "Religion and Politics" at Saint Joseph's University, a Catholic (Jesuit) university in Philadelphia. In the first weeks of class, as we read John Locke's *A Letter Concerning Toleration*, the president signed the executive order commonly referred to as the Muslim travel ban; the following month a Jewish cemetery in Philadelphia was desecrated. Not only was I emotionally stirred by these events, but I experienced intense cognitive dissonance between the seventeenth-century text about toleration we discussed in class and the events unfolding outside the classroom.

In the introduction to the course, we unpacked the writings of John Locke and William Penn and explored their influence on the American founders who crafted the United States Constitution. My class was surprised to discover that the First Amendment of the Constitution secures religious liberty first, before mentioning freedom of speech, freedom of the press, or the right to peaceably assemble. The American founders so prized protection for religious pluralism that they first enshrined into law the idea that there should be no single, established religion in the United States, and then the right of citizens to worship as they choose. I knew the narrative well. Yet how could I, in good conscience, teach this document in the face of recent events that seemed to call those convictions into question?

While I was not able to fully resolve this tension by the end of the class, it helped to have the American Values, Religious Voices letters to get us through the semester. After a local rabbi suggested that the class subscribe to the campaign, I made reading the letters a course requirement. At the time, I could not anticipate how the letters would bring the class comfort, connection, and clarity in the midst of those turbulent 100 days. While the 100 letters were addressed to "President Trump, Vice President Pence, Members of the Trump Administration and the 115th Congress," they had an impact on a much larger audience. This essay weaves together my personal experience reading the letters with my Saint Joseph's students with feedback from other campaign followers that Andrea Weiss collected from emails and social media posts during and after the 100 days.

. . . the mere fact of the authors joining their voices together into one powerful song demonstrated that religious pluralism was alive and well in the United States.

My course met three times a week, and we often started class by reading a letter. The text of the individual letters provided inspiration and insight, to be sure. But the mere fact of the authors joining their voices together into one powerful song demonstrated that religious pluralism was alive and well in the United States. The letters gave my class the opportunity to see democracy in action.

I remember reading certain letters aloud that caused my class to audibly gasp as the authors spoke truth to power in a seemingly prophetic way. Had we read some of the gasp-worthy statements just months earlier, they might have seemed as uncontroversial as a greeting card. However, in the context of the first 100 days of the Trump administration, those words stood out as bold critiques, what one campaign follower called a "glorious project in interreligious resistance" and another referred to as a "constructive part of our American response" to the 2016 election.

As a political scientist who studies American politics, I am well aware of the power of letters. John Locke wrote his letter on tolerance in 1685, addressed to his friend Philip von Limborch. Living in Amsterdam as a political exile, Locke could not openly express his views.

Even so, his letter was published anonymously and eventually lent ideological heft to the U.S. Constitution. The Reverend Dr. Martin Luther King Jr. also used the letter format when in 1963 he wrote what became known as the "Letter from Birmingham Jail." Though specifically addressed to "my dear fellow clergymen" in response to their critique of his actions, the letter reached a much wider audience and became one of the most important writings on civil disobedience in the American canon. Published letters are fascinating precisely because of this duality of audience.

Like the writings of Locke and King, the American Values, Religious Voices letters speak to those beyond their explicit audience. As my college students and I read these letters, we were cognizant of being part of a larger implicit audience, a growing group of followers who awaited the latest online letter each morning. This made us feel, as one reader shared, that we were "not alone." The feedback that came pouring in during the campaign reaffirms the experience of my Saint Joseph's class, demonstrating how readers responded to the wise, spiritual voices featured in the American Values, Religious Voices letters.

When the Founding Fathers drafted the Constitution, they tried to limit presidential powers as much as possible, for they viewed the executive branch as closely resembling a monarchy. Since the second article of the Constitution, which describes the executive branch, is shockingly short, much of the presidency is governed by unwritten norms that every president has followed. From the beginning, the Trump administration has deviated from some of these institutional norms. As a result of this and some of the executive actions, administrative appointments, tweets, and other events in President Trump's first months, many Americans experienced a heightened sense of anxiety and uncertainty during those first 100 days.

The feedback from American Values, Religious Voices followers testifies to both the emotional impact of that period and, in that context, the succor the letters provided. One reader expressed the hope that, over time, the voices in the letters would "begin to counterbalance those voices that cause so many of us pain these days." Just as an overseas follower characterized the campaign as "a lifeline to sanity these days," others described the letters as a daily "inoculation" against the news and "a balm on my heart and mind." Another follower found that the letters "run the gamut of being helpful, motivating,

> " These letters are short, focused, passionate, insightful, and filled with the presence of God. "

> " Often I have heard that the religious voice is missing in the broader conversation taking place in society. Your project proves that this is not the case. "

> " Thank you for bringing light into the darkness of our day. "

> " I find your efforts and the wisdom and kindness of the letters sustaining. "

inspirational and calming." Someone else elaborated: "In a time when I wake up each morning and go to bed each evening shaking my head in disbelief and horror upon hearing or reading the latest troubling quote from our new president, these letters serve as an anchor, a reminder of the quote that Dr. Martin Luther King Jr. shared so often, that 'the arc of the moral universe is long, but it bends towards justice.' " These and other responses made it clear that the letters served to assuage readers' fears and bring them some semblance of peace and stability.

American Values, Religious Voices made another powerful contribution by creating connections between faith traditions and between individuals: through authors who wrote letters and shared them on social media, readers who forwarded letters to family and friends and "liked" or retweeted them, clergy who recited the letters in worship services and interfaith gatherings, teachers who brought the letters to religious school classrooms, college campuses, and other communal gatherings. Alexis de Tocqueville noted in the nineteenth century that associations are critical to the health of society for many reasons, including the benefit of providing an alternative source of moral authority to the government. When government's moral authority seems compromised, such associations can become loci of leadership that exemplify another type of moral authority. American Values, Religious Voices provided a platform for this type of association by bringing together religious leaders who helped provide moral clarity. By joining their voices, the scholars who wrote the letters and the readers who discussed them amplified the critiques expressed in their individual communities, thus creating a shared commitment to speaking up, while providing a reminder that we are stronger when we listen to one another.

A sixth-grade teacher at a synagogue in New York City incorporated the letters into her social justice curriculum, much as a Presbyterian pastor in Auburn, Alabama, used the letters in a Sunday school class. When asked what made the letters effective, the kids in the Manhattan synagogue replied that using religious quotes helps "unite people who don't necessarily agree." These young people recognized that the letters provide "an example of how to talk to people when you want them to listen to what you have to say." Reflecting on the impact that day's lesson had on the students, the teacher

> " Thank you for the great learning you have given all of us. I hope the recipients in power are learning too. "

> " Thanks for making it so easy to share these wonderful letters. I am an atheist—BUT, that doesn't make me blind to good words and good advice. "

> " These letters . . . have simply been stellar, positive reminders of who we are, and encouragement to live boldly rather than out of fear. "

wrote: "They each felt validated in knowing that adults—professors and scholars—are feeling the same fear and doubt they are, and, perhaps more importantly, they felt reassured to know that these same people are actively working to combat those fears." After the students penned their own letters to the same recipients in Washington, "for the first time, they felt there was a way for them to add their own voices" to those speaking out about the issues that mattered most to them.

In a 2006 address to the American Academy of Religion, the scholar Diana Eck declared: "Pluralism takes the reality of difference as its starting point. The challenge of pluralism is not to obliterate or erase difference, nor to smooth out differences under a universalizing canopy, but rather to discover ways of living, connecting, relating, arguing and disagreeing in a society of differences." The American Values, Religious Voices campaign exemplifies that kind of pluralism. Writers drew from their own religious traditions and managed to forge deep connections to others out of that difference. One reader asserted: "The very existence of this site and this effort lies at the core of pluralism in our democracy." Another commented: "Not only are the letters wonderful for the advice they give to our leaders, but they are a very pithy statement of the core of our common faith." One follower, an atheist, admitted that even though she personally was not committed to a faith, she valued the project because of the "good works" and "good advice" it offered.

Although most of the feedback on American Values, Religious Voices was positive, the campaign had some critics. Each email from the relatively small number of people who wrote to take issue with certain aspects of the project received an authentic and gracious response from Andrea Weiss. Her replies often prompted additional correspondence, thus modeling peaceful, deliberative, democratic discourse. Instead of the culture war paradigm where different ideologies battle it out for one conquering dominant cultural hegemon, American Values, Religious Voices illustrates Eck's definition of pluralism: not obliterating difference, but "finding ways of living, connecting, relating, arguing and disagreeing in a society of differences."

One example comes from a reader who wrote to express her dismay that Letter 61 seemed to "reject religious pro-life arguments." The reader went on to describe herself: "For me as a pro-life feminist, political choices are increasingly difficult, as my conscience demands a pro-life stance as much as it demands a pro-refugee, pro-healthcare, pro–social justice, pro-environment, pro–gender equality, etc. stance." She continued: "I want to be involved in advocacy that protests against the very unfortunate political developments in the U.S. and Europe, but I feel alienated by the strong pro-choice element with which as a mother, Catholic and philosophically trained academic I cannot possibly align myself." Weiss' reply reaffirmed the aim of the project: "Diversity is at the heart of this campaign, as manifest in the diverse backgrounds of our writers and the diverse perspectives expressed. One of the strengths of the project is the variation in topic, tone and viewpoint." She added: "On Saturday we'll feature a letter from the Catholic theologian Shawnee Daniels-Sykes, who writes about the 'responsibility to uphold all human life with faith, hope and love.'" The reader wrote again the next day, full of gratitude: "Yes, of course I will continue reading the letters. My best wishes for the rest of your important and valuable project!" There are not many places in the United States right now where we can witness this kind of heartening exchange.

Abraham Lincoln once called the law the "political religion" of the United States. If we take his words as truth, I imagine the American Founding Fathers would have been gratified that the "sacred text" of the First Amendment was so well interpreted in word and deed by the writers of the American Values, Religious Voices campaign. The project helped me better square my understanding of religion and politics as I taught during the first 100 days of the Trump administration. Now, through this book, the letters can continue to inspire hope, provide comfort, create community, and support those who believe in deliberative democracy, pluralism, and the power of religious voices speaking out, reminding us of our shared American values.

" I wanted to again write you a note thanking you for the post inauguration project. It is wisdom and hope in my e-mail every day. It brings me living waters of sustenance and courage from deep ancient wells. "

AUTHORS' POSTSCRIPT

Raising Our Voices and Reflecting on Our Values

By Hussein Rashid

Independent Scholar & Founder, islamicate, L3C

Andrea Weiss emailed me on December 1, 2016, and invited me to participate in the nascent American Values, Religious Voices: 100 Days, 100 Letters campaign. She asked me not just to write a letter, but to join the advisory committee. She framed the request this way: "Just as our list of letter writers will be diverse in terms of religion, race, gender, sexual orientation, political affiliation, geography, etc., we would like the advisory committee to reflect that diversity." Since I thought the goal was laudable, she did not need to do much convincing. After some back-and-forth on what my role would be, I gladly joined her merry group of scholars.

We cemented the deal the first time we met over an afternoon snack at a diner in midtown Manhattan. We played "six degrees of Muslim-Jewish separation," figuring out who we knew in common, which even in a city of about eight million people is quite a few in our line of work. That interaction affirmed my interest in the project. In many ways, that meeting at the diner reflected what I hope for these sorts of engagements. Two individuals can start with points of agreement

> *Two individuals can start with points of agreement and then delve deeper into differences in a respectful way, thinking about how to build on the points we have in common.*

and then delve deeper into differences in a respectful way, thinking about how to build on the points we have in common. We can do this because we are part of a community of good will and because we see ourselves as being called to our better natures, as the Qur'an says, to "compete in good works" (2:148). This worldview has been shaped by the New York I grew up in, and it shapes the United States I want to see now and in the future.

Looking back at that initial conversation and the letter writing campaign that followed, we can consider what American Values, Religious Voices accomplished.

One year after the conclusion of the campaign, we asked the letter writers to reflect on their participation in the project and its impact. We asked them to consider why they selected the topic of their letter and what they see as the continued relevance of the issues they raised. The authors' reflections serve as a collective postscript to the 100 letters.

RAISING OUR VOICES

From the outset, diversity was an important goal of this project. The vision was broad both in theory and in practice, for it sought to include scholars who were not just academics, but theologians and community leaders. While a few of these voices were starting to gain prominence in the pre-Trump era, many were new to a more public arena. For Deirdre Good (Letter 42), one noteworthy aspect of the campaign was the way the letters provided "daily evidence of religious scholars offering hope and wisdom by visibly leading in public." She observed: "Taken together, our letters stand as witness to the public voice of scholars not just at a particular time and place, but from religious traditions central to the lives of our people." Likewise, for Karoline Lewis (Letter 74), the campaign "brought to light the importance and consequences of being a public theologian and underscored the desperate need for those willing to speak up about and speak into the shaping of moral imagination." According to Patrick Reyes (Letter 48), the letters "remind us of the collective power and responsibility of public religious leadership" as they "honor and advance the prophetic, spiritual, intellectual, and moral line of global faith leaders."

Several letter writers commented on what it meant to speak out publicly at this moment in history. Shalom Holtz (Letter 20) wrote: "Being part of American Values, Religious Voices has meant that my voice is included among those who did not stand by in silence as our way of life was completely upended in the 2016 election. We have gone on record as being on the right, moral side of history." Emran El-Badawi (Letter 29) expressed a similar sentiment when he noted: "Adding my voice to ninety-nine distinguished colleagues across America sends a powerful message during a rather dark period in our country's history. America is more divided now than I can ever remember. . . . But we did not remain silent." He declared: "This campaign allowed the world to see that leading American academics stand for justice and against hate."

Explaining why he accepted the invitation to write a letter, Marc Brettler (Letter 14) stated: "Like many others, I felt powerless and was looking for any possible outlet through which I could express my feelings of impending disaster—disaster for the county, especially for its most vulnerable inhabitants. I shared the premises of the project—that religious texts and traditions are important and can be comforting, and perhaps even powerful, persuasive voices at times of crisis. I was excited to be one voice, representing one slice of one tradition, among many other writers and traditions."

UNITY AND DIVERSITY

Like Brettler, other authors found it meaningful to be part of a multifaith collection of scholars bringing their religious teachings to bear on current events. Murali Balaji (Letter 36) optimistically asserted: "I have been heartened to see how communities of faith are working together to envision a more pluralistic America. I remain more confident than ever that through our

" . . . we have to reach across the aisle, respect, listen, and learn."

– JOHN KUTSKO

"America is more divided now than I can ever remember. . . . But we did not remain silent."

– EMRAN EL-BADAWI

" . . . we call ourselves, we call our society, back to healing through the deep wisdom of our sacred traditions."

– GREG CAREY

" 'American values' are not the domain of any one group."

– ESTHER HAMORI

"Regardless of whether one is religious or not, drawing upon the wisdom of humanity's sacred texts and the ethical teachings of mystics, sages, and visionaries allows us to invoke enduring truths amidst constant flux."

– ZAYN KASSAM

" . . . I sensed encouragement percolating through a project that was determined to promote the existence of common ground . . . "

– MATTHEW SKINNER

" Contributing to . . . the project has enabled me to participate in this larger conversation about who we are as a nation, who we want to be, and the legacy we will leave future generations."

– LISA BOWENS

"They are more than letters . . . They are a religious cry for public servants to see how interconnected our global lives are and what the wisdom our religious and spiritual traditions offer for this moment."

– PATRICK REYES

many voices, one future will emerge." Similarly, Tamara Eskenazi (Letter 26) noted how she "found affirmation in the potential of a shared vision in the midst of valued differences."

John Kutsko (Letter 2) captured this interplay of unity and diversity when he warned that the Bill of Rights protects "our deepest differences only if we are willing to focus on our deepest shared values. To protect our own rights, we need to protect those of others." Emphasizing the importance of compromise—the topic addressed in his letter—Kutsko argued: "We all care about education, immigration, social services, health care, safety and security, and jobs and the economy. Those are common goals and shared values. But unless we have leadership that respects each other, that engages in conversation, and that focuses on common ground, then the common good will not be served and our common goals will not be reached." For that to happen, he advocates, "we have to reach across the aisle, respect, listen, and learn."

A MULTIPLICITY OF VOICES AND VALUES

Reflecting on the personal impact of the campaign, Lisa Bowens (Letter 5) observed: "We live in a critical time when we have to decide what kind of nation we are going to be and what kind of values we want to embody and exhibit before the world. Contributing to the American Values, Religious Voices project has enabled me to participate in this larger conversation about who we are as a nation, who we want to be, and the legacy we will leave future generations."

As Esther Hamori (Letter 73) pointed out, there is no consensus about the values explored in this conversation. She wrote: "I appreciated the opportunity

. . . many of the people who wrote for this project do not look like the politicians to whom they addressed their letters and who are making decisions. Instead, they look more like the people who are affected by the decisions those politicians make.

to be part of a project that reflects that 'American values' are not the domain of any one group." Her comment reminds us that there is no static vision of what it means to be "American"; therefore, "American values" remain contested and contentious.

In light of the complex makeup of the United States, we are identified by race, religion, sexuality, class, gender, and fandom. Our letter writers only hint at the diverse ways in which Americans live. Yet it should be noted that many of the people who wrote for this project do not look like the politicians to whom they addressed their letters and who are making decisions. Instead, they look more like the people who are affected by the decisions those politicians make. This difference is not accidental. The disparity reflects the reality of our current political system, which still privileges the rich white male as the epitome of citizenship and power, even though the face of America is now radically different. For many of us, it is our lives that are at stake, not political victories. Our bodies are tied to our race, and sometimes that is tied to our religion.

Patrick Reyes touched upon this point when he reminded us: "The stakes are high for religious leaders of color and our allies, because the conditions we face are a matter of life and death." He framed the letters this way: "They are more than letters to the leaders of the United States. They are a religious cry for public servants to see how interconnected our global lives are and what wisdom our religious and spiritual traditions offer for this moment." When this cry is effective, religions provide a needed moral critique. We can see American Values, Religious Voices as a promise of what America could be. We do not want a country as it has been, with structures of oppression and marginalization built into its systems. Rather, we want the promise of what we could be. We are grounded in hope and strive to realize that hope.

HEALING AND HOPE

For Greg Carey (Letter 53), the 100 letters stand as a "witness." He asserted: "Mendacity, corruption, bigotry and ill will still raise our blood pressure and diminish our sleep. Yet we call ourselves, we call our society, back to healing through the deep wisdom of our sacred traditions. True transformation requires this spiritual core." Carey explained that since he wanted to make a positive contribution to our public discourse, he "chose to write in a spirit of hope"; and, in the end, he found most helpful the letters that projected that same sense of hope.

We can, perhaps, begin that process of healing by naming the diseases that infect our social fabric, as some letters do. However, naming racism, misogyny, xenophobia, homophobia, transphobia, and other ills that plague our country is not sufficient. We also need to offer a way forward. We must act as well as think and feel.

The importance of hope and the need for words to lead to action came through as Nirinjan Kaur Khalsa (Letter 85) reflected on the impact of this project: "At a time of darkness, fear, anger, and distrust, this campaign has offered a beacon of light and hope. By raising our voices and calling upon the wisdom of our religious traditions we are reminded to learn from the lessons of the past, to look inward and to the divine so that we may have the courage to fight tyranny and oppression with love and unity." Amir Hussain (Letter 46) likewise linked words and actions when he wrote: "What was, and remains, important for me with the American Values, Religious Voices project was the various interfaith voices speaking together. . . . We need to work together, to make this a better country for all of us." For Forrest Clingerman (Letter 93), "hope is founded on the critical, constructive, and vital engagement that is emerging in response to the dusty old halls of power," particularly as exhibited by young people across the country.

COMMUNITY AND SOLIDARITY

Matthew Skinner (Letter 49) explained how the campaign gave him a sense of hope and a feeling of community: "Although the format of the project did not allow for back-and-forth conversations among the contributors, still I learned much and found my own perspectives enlarged simply by reading about others' efforts to grapple with similar questions. Especially at a time when fragmentation and frustration appear to be spiking in American society, I sensed encouragement percolating through a project that was determined to promote the existence of common ground and to make a statement that religious texts and traditions bear a

*Despite our best intentions,
we cannot achieve perfection;
yet we can strive for
a more perfect union.*

proven and practical wisdom for us to heed now, when vital social values are disintegrating."

Skinner called attention to the sense of solidarity provided by the letters when he wrote: "I suspect that the campaign mostly reached and encouraged people whose political and religious views already gave high value to generosity, diversity, peacemaking, the common good, and environmental justice. Nevertheless, the 100 letters reminded those people that they were not alone." He concluded: "If American Values, Religious Voices provided an impetus for religious communities to direct their energies toward an alternate vision of 'greatness' in America, and if it encouraged those communities to seek new partners in doing so, then the project was more than worth the effort."

For Zayn Kassam (Letter 94), the letters provided not only solidarity, but stability. She stated: "Regardless of whether one is religious or not, drawing upon the wisdom of humanity's sacred texts and the ethical teachings of mystics, sages, and visionaries allows us to invoke enduring truths amidst constant flux." Perhaps it was the political moment of the first 100 days of the Trump administration, as we responded to an assault on our very ideas of who we are as people, that proved to those writing and reading the letters how much our

different religious traditions could offer in what many experienced as a time of confusion, crisis, and loss.

A COMMON TESTIMONY

Eric Barreto (Letter 3) captured the spirit of many of our authors when he declared: "The work of advocating for God's justice remains unfinished. My hope is that these 100 letters are a common testimony of shared hopes in the midst of a politics that more often divides us, a politics that nurtures in us a sense that we are involved in a zero-sum game of winners and losers. The faiths of the letter writers suggest something quite different. The abundance of God's world and grace are a guarantee that we live in the midst of plenty. The question before us is how we will be wise and faithful stewards of such abundant gifts."

Through the American Values, Religious Voices campaign, we are generating the type of common testimony Barreto describes. We are struggling together and exploring how we can create a better whole. At the same time, we know that we are failing—such is the human condition. Growth can only happen when we recognize that we will make mistakes and that we must rectify them. This collection of 100 letters does not include every faith tradition, nor does it include people who profess no faith. Yet we are all part of the same community. Even in our inclusive vision, there are blind spots, some of which we are aware of, and some which we are not.

Despite our best intentions, we cannot achieve perfection; yet we can strive for a more perfect union. We acknowledge our limits and invite you to join us in a conversation aimed to make us all better, as individuals and as a nation. There is a diner in New York where we can meet.

A PRAYER
FOR OUR COUNTRY

Every inch of America is sacred, from sea to shining sea.

There is much to be done in our time, the sort of hard work on which God smiles
because it is done for the sake of the dignity and well-being of all God's creatures.

Together, let us work to preserve and make manifest the
values upon which our democracy was founded.

The task of all people of faith is to call governing authorities to
fulfill God's purpose of bringing about justice, mercy, and peace.

Individually and as a nation, may we heed our obligations
to each other as we navigate the tensions of building a just society.

Rather than a politics of divisiveness, may we move our country toward a politics of empathy.

May we use our power well so we do great things for all God's creatures,
all those made in God's image who yearn for an equal place at America's table.

If we do all this, may grace and peace be ours in abundance.
May we be a beacon and a blessing to the world.

· ·

Compiled and adapted from American Values, Religious Voices letters by
Eboo Patel, Jean-Pierre Ruiz, Andrea Weiss, Susan Garrett, Carmen Nanko-Fernández,
Aristotle Papanikolaou, Katharine R. Henderson, M. Craig Barnes

★ ACKNOWLEDGMENTS ★

Over the past twenty years, scholars' publishing options have increased dramatically. While information found on the internet may not be peer reviewed or stable, it nonetheless competes with university press books for readers' attention, allowing them to consume more information more quickly than ever before. As a university press publisher of social justice scholarship and dialogue, my goal is to find manuscripts which engage and impact the global community, connecting scholars to practitioners and the lay community in order to disseminate new ideas and methods to solve real-world common problems.

Hebrew Union College–Jewish Institute of Religion and University of Cincinnati sit on perpendicular streets in the Clifton district of Cincinnati and have enjoyed a close, collaborative relationship for nearly 145 years. So on a rainy day in February 2018, I met with incoming HUC-JIR Provost, Andrea Weiss. Toward the end of the conversation, almost as an afterthought, I asked Andrea if she had plans to write a book. She then told me about a post-election social media campaign that she created with her friend, graphic designer Lisa Weinberger, called American Values, Religious Voices: 100 Days, 100 Letters. Nearly a year after the campaign ended, they sought a different vehicle to preserve the letters and bring them to a larger audience. I was immediately taken with the opportunity to engage with Andrea, Lisa, and the letter writers and to explore new ways to present the letters. Together, we began to strategize about a book.

Our goals were simple: invite the contributors to reflect on the project in an authors' postscript, create a design that reflected the visual identity of the online campaign and enhanced its beauty, showcase values in the complied letters, and demonstrate how the book could serve as a resource for personal insight and inspiration, or for homilies, teaching, interfaith gatherings, and more. We wanted the book out by the midterm elections in November 2018, and at an affordable price. Despite busy schedules, we each knew what we had to do. Within months of our first planning meeting, I was at the New York Review of Books and BookExpo America talking about this book as part of our debut season. This project was a challenge for a brand new publisher, but one I could not pass by.

As I write this today at my desk on the uptown campus of UC, about to publish our first season of books, I am incredibly proud to have *American Values, Religious Voices: 100 Days, 100 Letters* on the list. I am humbled that Andrea Weiss and Lisa Weinberger took a chance on our tiny publishing operation. The journey we—a scholar, designer, and publisher—undertook has been rewarding, collaborative, and exciting. We have created a model of how Americans can find common themes amidst our diversity. I am honored to bring to readers this collection of letters and essays written by scholars from across the country who represent an array of religions: authors who are Muslim, Buddhist, Hindu, Sikh, Christian, and Jewish.

I encourage you to share your thoughts about this book on Twitter at @ucincipress and @valuesandvoices and on our University of Cincinnati Press Facebook and Instagram pages. Tag us, tweet us, and invite us to join your reading or discussion groups, whether they be in a house of worship, an institution of learning, or some other setting. The editors, authors, and I are available virtually or in person to continue this conversation about core American values.

Elizabeth Scarpelli
Director, University of Cincinnati Press
and Library Publisher Services

★ ACKNOWLEDGMENTS ★

Neither this book nor the American Values, Religious Voices campaign would have happened if my dear friend Lisa Weinberger had not responded "I'm in" when I asked for her help with my farfetched post-election idea. Elsa Dixler, one of our copy editors, captured the depth of our collaborative partnership when she observed that "this book is among other things a testament to the friendship between you and Lisa."

As I explain in my essay "Raising 100 Voices," a number of other people played pivotal roles in this project. Hebrew Union College–Jewish Institute of Religion President Rabbi Aaron D. Panken, of blessed memory, financed the campaign and championed the project at every opportunity. It is only fitting that this book is dedicated to him. I thank Jean Bloch Rosensaft, HUC-JIR assistant vice president for communications and public affairs, and Allison Glazer, assistant director, who energetically publicized the campaign and now are helping us promote the book.

I express my heartfelt gratitude to the members of the advisory committee: Deirdre Good, Herbert Marbury, Hussein Rashid, Mark Smith, and Elsie Stern. Deirdre and Hussein were often the first ones in the morning to retweet and forward the daily social media posts. We have had opportunities to speak about the campaign at various events, a further sign of their dedication to this project. I also thank our terrific HUC-JIR rabbinic student interns, Hilly Haber and Thalia Halpert Rodis, who eagerly threw themselves into the campaign and helped us establish and maintain a strong social media presence.

My family was incredibly supportive and understanding as the campaign took shape. My husband, Alan Tauber, picked up the slack at home and became one of our most loyal Twitter followers. My son, Ilan, cheered me on daily and adjusted to many nights of take-out dinners. My daughter, Rebecca, followed the campaign from afar while on a gap year and, on Day 100, posted one of the most meaningful comments I received: "So lucky to have a mom who accomplishes such amazing things and teaches me what initiative and hard work can achieve." For the book, she helped edit the essays and index.

My siblings were among our most committed followers. For their love and encouragement, I thank Mitchell, Laura, and Roger Weiss, his wife, Catherine Corrigan, Michele and Mark Tauber, plus my parents Marty and Ruth Weiss and Arthur and Jean Tauber. I also thank my many friends who subscribed to the letters and supported me for the 100 days and beyond.

An unexpected meeting with the University of Cincinnati Press in February 2018, led to this publication. I am immensely grateful to Elizabeth Scarpelli, press and publishing services director, Sarah Muncy, editorial assistant, and the others at UC Press who recognized the potential of this project and worked hard to produce a spectacular book. Thanks also go to our copy editors, Janice Fisher and Elsa Dixler, and our indexer, HUC-JIR rabbinic and education student Vanessa Harper.

And last but certainly not least, the campaign owes its success both to the 100 authors who said "yes" and wrote to our leaders in Washington with passion, insight, and vision rooted in their religious traditions, and to our readers, who not only followed the campaign but became part of the dialogue by sharing the letters with others and their feedback with us.

In Letter 14, Marc Brettler writes: "Standing idly by, or arguing that someone else should step up, is not an option. We are each accountable if we do not work to improve our communities." American Values, Religious Voices has been my way of stepping up.

Andrea L. Weiss

★ ACKNOWLEDGMENTS ★

I must first acknowledge my twenty-three years of friendship with the creator of this campaign, Andrea Weiss. It's because of our bond and my deep admiration for her imaginative idea that I agreed to do a design "favor" of this scope. She is a true believer in the power of collaboration. Her commitment to unite not just a biblical scholar, a designer, and 100 people of faith, but all people who treasure what we stand for as Americans, was my inspiration. Andrea kept the campaign fire burning with an infectious passion that even a year and a half later is manifest in the creation of this book.

I'm grateful to my colleague Roni Lagin who graciously accepted my invitation to participate as a member of the design team. I handed off a meager suite of graphic elements, and in record-breaking time he magically crafted a beautiful website. His instinct to design with clarity enabled tens of thousands of people to gain access to the letters.

Benjamin Brown, Vicki Gray-Wolfe, and Matthew Muhlbaier, my remarkable staff at Masters Group Design, played a significant role during the campaign, not the least of which was willingly taking on my other projects so I could give the campaign my singular focus. They lent their creative expertise to the website and the development of all visual assets—for online use and this book. The newest addition to our team, Brielle Gall, was a key player in the production of this publication, from typesetting to image editing. I am deeply blessed to have co-workers who embrace the spirit of teamwork.

My clients were especially supportive during my semi-absence as the campaign was afoot. Their words of encouragement and willingness to advertise the website on their organizations' social media and in their newsletters proved to me that "partners" is a far better name for Masters Group Design's loyal base.

To my family and friends who supported my "love project," thank you. My friend Wendy Weiss deserves a special acknowledgment for allowing my endless campaign ramblings to dominate the conversation during our weekly coffee meet-ups. For months she was a patient and kind listener.

I'm indebted to my fabulous parents, Norman and Susan Weinberger, who taught me the importance of being engaged and giving back. Their encouragement of my design activism grounded me through this project. They read every letter, followed the campaign "religiously" (to quote my mom) and even spotted typos that in our exhaustion we were incapable of seeing.

My husband, Eric, and sons, Avi and Jakob, deserve my love and appreciation. They let me roll freely with no demands while I immersed myself in a campaign that rendered me unavailable for long stretches of time.

Andrea framed the campaign under the motto that, "Individually, it is hard to feel that one can have an impact. Collectively, we have the potential to speak more powerfully." This book is nothing without the inspired words of the authors who crafted such heartfelt letters. Thank you for joining together in this meaningful way and for modeling the kind of unity that makes me proud to be an American.

I am humbled by the University of Cincinnati Press' interest in this book, not just as an important record of the times but as a collective voice that speaks with more than just words.

Lisa M. Weinberger

Scriptural Index

Subject Index

commandment: 31, 56, 80, 89, 119, 125–26
commitment: 47–48, 55, 56, 70, 83, 94, 119, 137, 149
community: 16, 28, 30, 32, 34, 42, 47, 51, 55–56, 66–67, 79, 82, 91–92, 102–3, 105, 108, 112, 114–15, 125–26, 139, 144, 149, 150, 152–53, 156–57, 159
compassion: 10, 16–17, 19, 23, 31–32, 35, 45, 54, 60, 65, 67, 72, 76–77, 89, 92, 94, 101, 117, 125–26, 130, 132, 135, 144
compromise: 28, 45, 70, 100, 155
Confucianism: 132
Confucius: 90
conscience: 36, 55, 99, 132, 142–43, 146, 150
Constitution of the United States: 28, 52, 91, 96, 100, 118, 135, 138, 146–47
Coolidge, Calvin: 64
courage: 19, 29, 126–27, 129, 151, 156
covenant: 58, 70
creation: 17, 30, 40, 47, 58, 70–71, 75, 78, 84, 141; creation of

humans in God's image: 17, 40, 65, 69, 75, 89, 104, 114; humans created equally: 29, 84, 91
Cruz, Jeremy V: 98, 108

D
Daniels–Sykes, Shawnee M: 98, 104
Dávila, Maria Teresa: 122, 124
Day, Dorothy: 82, 93
DeAnda, Neomi: 98, 105
debate: 28, 70, 96
Declaration of Independence: 17, 91
Delgado, Teresa: 86, 93
democracy: 18–19, 27–28, 39, 68, 70–71, 77, 92, 100, 129, 135, 139, 142, 147, 150, 158
deportation: 78, 84, 105, 108, 119, 139
determination: 39, 66, 116
Dhanidina, Halim: 140
Díaz, Miguel H: 86, 92
dignity: 27, 34, 41, 45, 47, 55, 58, 75, 104, 113,

136, 141, 158
disability: 41, 47, 92, 94, 115
disagreements: 19, 39, 51, 54, 81, 100, 150
dissent: 36, 120, 142
diversity: 8, 12–13, 16, 18, 20, 28, 33, 59, 100–1, 104, 111, 140, 144, 150, 152–53, 155, 157
divisions: 19, 43, 54, 66, 69, 88, 104
dream: 39, 83, 106, 129; American Dream: 32, 39, 116; DREAMers: 47
Dreisbach, Daniel L: 27, 130

E
e pluribus unum: 28, 116, 145
earth: 17, 39, 42, 47, 63, 71, 75, 81, 91, 93, 102, 106, 108, 130, 137–38, 142
Easter: 15, 119–20, 129, 139
Eck, Diana: 149–50
economy: 42–43, 59, 66, 68, 71–72, 78, 84, 87, 94–95, 108, 115, 119, 125, 130, 137–38,

155
education: 60, 82, 84, 155
Eisenhower, Dwight D: 64
El–Badawi, Emran: 50, 59, 153–54
Ellison, Keith: 140
Eltantawi, Sarah: 110, 112
empathy: 8, 16, 20, 27, 41, 68, 136, 158
environment: 16, 46–47, 84, 137–38, 150, 157
equality: 8, 16, 29, 118, 127, 150
Eskenazi, Tamara Cohn: 49–50, 56, 155

F
family: 16, 33, 43–44, 67, 69, 78–80, 82, 84, 91, 99, 102, 104–5, 124, 126, 132, 143–44, 148
Faried, Kenneth: 140
fear: 23, 29, 35, 40–41, 43, 54, 57, 60, 77–78, 97, 104, 115, 118, 127–28, 139, 148–49, 156
Flake, Kathleen: 122, 131
Flynn, Michael: 112
Founding Fathers: 27,

59, 100, 130, 147, 150
Franklin, Benjamin: 60
freedom: 9, 29, 34,
44–45, 63, 69, 70, 83,
87, 90, 92, 94, 116, 124,
127, 129–30, 139, 141;
freedom of assembly:
33, 77, 146; **freedom
of the press**: 77, 146;
freedom of religion:
29–30, 33, 36, 44, 69, 77,
94, 99–100, 103, 111,
127, 146; **freedom of
speech**: 29, 77, 141, 146
future: 13, 31, 54,
59, 66, 71, 82, 87, 94,
118–19, 126, 138–39,
152, 154–55

G

Gall, Brielle: 132, 161
Gámez, Daisy Flores:
105
**Gandhi, Mahatma
(Mohandas)**: 17, 45, 93
Gargallo, Pablo: 47
Garrett, Susan R: 74,
81, 158
Garroway, Joshua D:
50, 60
generosity: 11, 32,
44–45, 57–58, 65, 76,
107, 126, 131, 139, 157
God: 12, 17, 23, 27, 29,

30–31, 34, 36, 40–42,
44, 46, 48, 51, 53–54,
56–58, 60, 69, 70–72, 75,
80–81, 83, 89, 92–93, 96,
99, 102–5, 111, 114–15,
118, 123, 127–31, 135,
137–38, 140–42, 144,
148, 157–58
Golden Rule: 56, 64
Goleman, Daniel: 88
Good, Deirdre: 13, 74,
76, 153, 160
good, the: 27, 30, 66,
68, 70, 80, 96, 107, 118,
123, 138, 143; **common
good**: 11, 18, 28, 34, 39,
45–46, 111, 135, 139,
143–44, 155, 157; **good
news**: 29, **63**, **87**, 104,
129; **good Samaritan**:
31, 65; **goodwill**: 101,
152; **greater good**: 30,
76, **100**, 138; **goodness**:
90, 118, 132, 135, 141
grace: 29, 31, 43, 129,
157–58
gratitude: 22, 57, 91,
103, 150
Gray–Wolfe, Vicki: 13,
23, 97, 161
greatness: 32, 45,
111, 124, 144, 157;
**"Make America Great
Again"**: 104, 111
Guru Gobind Singh:

127
Guru Nanak: 55, 127

H

Halal Guys: 140
Hammer, Fannie Lou:
82, 108
Hamori, Esther J:
110, 113, 154–55
Hanh, Thich Nhat: 93
happiness: 111, 117,
135, 139
hard work: 29, 34, 39,
104, 158, 159
hate: 35, 41, 54, 65,
77, 82, 97, 108, 127,
140, 153; **hatred**: 55,
57, 59, 84, 104, 112,
141
Haws, J. B: 98, 102
Hayes, Christine:
73–75
healing: 19, 20, 46, 54,
91, 101, 118, 138, 154,
156
health care: 47, 60, 82,
84, 139, 143, 150, 155
Held, Shai: 134, 141
Helwys, Thomas: 36
**Henderson,
Katharine R**: 50–51,
158
**Heschel, Abraham
Joshua**: 82, 93, 141

Hidalgo, Jacqueline M:
62, 66
Hindu(s): 16–17, 45,
68, 116, 144
**Hogan, Karina
Martin**: 38, 44
holiness: 54, 125, 139
Holtz, Shalom E: 38,
48, 153
homophobia: 112, 156
honor: 41, 47–48,
55, 59, 63, 82, 87–89,
91–92, 105, 107, 111,
124–25, 136, 141, 153
hope: 10, 19, 20, 29,
36, 39, 46, 51–52, 66–
67, 87–88, 90, 104, 106,
113, 117, 119–20, 125,
129, 135, 137, 139, 143,
148, 150–53, 156–57
hospitality: 11, 17, 41,
46, 67, 83, 87, 91, 119,
121, 124, 144
Hughes, Langston:
17, 108, 111
Hultgren, Randy: 19
humanity: 40, 55, 58,
65, 71–72, 75, 83–84,
100, 112–14, 119,
126–27, 136, 154, 157
humility: 11, 18, 48,
72, 76, 79, 80, 88, 90,
107, 136, 139, 142, 144
Hussain, Amir: 74,
80, 156

61, 91, 150
Locke, John: 146–47
love: 10, 16–17, 27, 31, 35, 41, 43–44, 47, 49, 51, 54–57, 65, 67, 71–72, 76, 80, 82, 87, 90, 97, 104–5, 114, 117, 119, 123, 125–27, 136, 138, 150, 156
loyalty: 44, 56, 70, 143
Luke: 31, 53, 81, 87, 94

M
Majeed, Debra: 134, 140
Malden, Massachusetts: 124
Marbury, Herbert R: 13, 134, 143, 160
Mary: 102
Massingale, Bryan N: 19, 50, 54, 61
Matthew: 35, 64, 76, 93
McGuire, Katherine: 19
Mehta, Narsi: 45
Mencius: 132
mercy: 8, 27, 31, 65, 79–81, 87, 90, 101–2, 129, 131, 136, 158
migrants: 17, 47, 64, 101, 104–5, 123
military: 47, 53, 64, 82, 108, 131

Miller, Althea Spencer: 62, 70
Miriam: 103, 124
misogyny: 40, 101, 112, 114, 156
Molina, Evelia Quintana: 105
Moltmann, Jürgen: 67
Mormon(s): 33, 36, 102, 131
Moses: 35, 60, 89, 95, 124, 142
Mott, Lucretia: 126
Muhammad (The Prophet): 30, 136
Muir, John: 137
Muslim(s): 16–17, 30, 33, 36, 39, 41, 44, 51, 59, 78, 80, 111–13, 118, 135–36, 140, 142, 144, 146, 152

N
Nadella, Raj: 86, 94
Nanko-Fernández, Carmen: 38, 47, 158
Nasrallah, Laura: 74, 79
Native American(s): 16, 31, 78, 104, 143–44
neighbor: 17, 31, 43, 54, 56, 65, 80, 92, 108, 117, 119, 125, 137, 139, 140
New Testament: 17,

44, 63, 76, 79, 80, 87, 106, 114, 128

O
Obama, Barack: 64
Odeh, Fadia: 140
Old Testament: 17, 28
Orthodox Christians/ Church: 28, 41, 120
outsiders: 31, 33, 78, 83

P
Paine, Thomas: 27
Panken, Aaron D: 12, 74, 84, 160
Papanikolaou, Aristotle: 38, 41, 158
parables: 31, 64, 94, 101, 106, 115, 120
Passover: 22, 119, 121, 123, 144
Patel, Eboo: 38–39, 158
patience: 76, 118
Paul: 66, 76, 81, 94, 102, 139
peace: 9, 34, 36, 43, 47, 51, 57, 69, 76, 80–81, 93, 95, 104, 111, 116–17, 131, 136, 139, 148, 157–58
Penn, William: 146
Pentecost: 104, 144
Peppard, Michael: 15,

26, 33
Pharaoh: 59, 124, 142
Plaskow, Judith: 17, 74, 78
Pledge of Allegiance: 17, 58
pluralism: 9, 28, 36, 39, 59, 84, 118, 146–47, 149, 150, 153
poor, the: 42–45, 53, 60, 63–64, 72, 82, 87, 89, 94–95, 101, 104, 130, 143; **poverty**: 47, 68–69, 128
Pope Francis: 34, 92–93, 105
Pope John Paul II: 54
Pope Paul VI: 46, 93
power: 19, 29, 32, 41, 45, 47–48, 51–53, 55, 57, 63, 69, 72, 75–78, 81–82, 84, 87–88, 90, 94, 101, 103, 107, 123, 127–29, 141–43, 145, 147, 149–50, 153, 155–56, 158
prayer: 17–18, 68, 89, 103, 111, 142, 158
privilege: 29, 36, 92, 94, 107, 116, 125, 130, 141, 155
progress: 29, 68, 115
promise: 39, 91, 111, 118, 120, 135, 138, 143, 156
prophets: 27, 29–30,

COLLECTIVELY,

may we all speak truthfully and powerfully
to those making critical decisions
about our nation's future.

Notes

☆

⋆

☆

100 Days, 100 Letters